11/06

L.M. Montgomery

WHO
WROTE
THAT?

WHO
WROTE
THAT?

L.M. Montgomery

Marylou Morano Kjelle

Foreword by
Kyle Zimmer

CHELSEA HOUSE
PUBLISHERS
A Haights Cross Communications ✦ Company ®
Philadelphia

CHELSEA HOUSE PUBLISHERS

VP, New Product Development   Sally Cheney
Director of Production   Kim Shinners
Creative Manager   Takeshi Takahashi
Manufacturing Manager   Diann Grasse

Staff for L.M. MONTGOMERY

Executive Editor   Matt Uhler
Editorial Assistant   Sarah Sharpless
Production Editor   Noelle Nardone
Photo Editor   Sarah Bloom
Series Designer   Keith Trego
Layout   21st Century Publishing and Communications, Inc.

First Printing

1 3 5 7 9 8 6 4 2

Library of Congress Cataloging-in-Publication Data

Kjelle, Marylou Morano.
   Lucy Maud Montgomery/Marylou Morano Kjelle.
      p. cm.—(Who wrote that?)
   ISBN 0-7910-8234-2 (alk. paper)
   1. Montgomery, L. M. (Lucy Maud), 1874–1942. 2. Novelists, Canadian—
20th century—Biography. I. Title. II. Series.
PR9199.3.M6Z765 2004
813'.52—dc22
                                                            2004022350

All links and Web addresses were checked and verified to be correct at the time
of publication. Because of the dynamic nature of the Web, some addresses
and links may have changed since publication and may no longer be valid.

Table of Contents

FOREWORD BY
KYLE ZIMMER
PRESIDENT, FIRST BOOK

HUMANITY IS POWERED by stories. From our earliest days as thinking beings, we employed every available tool to tell each other stories. We danced, drew pictures on the walls of our caves, spoke, and sang. All of this extraordinary effort was designed to entertain, recount the news of the day, explain natural occurrences—and then gradually to build religious and cultural traditions and establish the common bonds and continuity that eventually formed civilizations. Stories are the most powerful force in the universe; they are the primary element that has distinguished our evolutionary path.

Our love of the story has not diminished with time. Enormous segments of societies are devoted to the art of storytelling. Book sales in the United States alone topped $26 billion last year; movie studios spend fortunes to create and promote stories; and the news industry is more pervasive in its presence than ever before.

There is no mystery to our fascination. Great stories are magic. They can introduce us to new cultures, or remind us of the nobility and failures of our own, inspire us to greatness or scare us to death; but above all, stories provide human insight on a level that is unavailable through any other source. In fact, stories connect each of us to the rest of humanity not just in our own time, but also throughout history.

This special magic of books is the greatest treasure that we can hand down from generation to generation. In fact, that spark in a child that comes from books became the motivation for the creation of my organization, First Book, a national literacy program with a simple mission: to provide new books to the most disadvantaged children. At present, First Book has been at work in hundreds of communities for over a decade. Every year children in need receive millions of books through our organization and millions more are provided through dedicated literacy institutions across the United States and around the world. In addition, groups of people dedicate themselves tirelessly to working with children to share reading and stories in every imaginable setting from schools to the streets. Of course, this Herculean effort serves many important goals. Literacy translates to productivity and employability in life and many other valid and even essential elements. But at the heart of this movement are people who love stories, love to read, and want desperately to ensure that no one misses the wonderful possibilities that reading provides.

When thinking about the importance of books, there is an overwhelming urge to cite the literary devotion of great minds. Some have written of the magnitude of the importance of literature. Amy Lowell, an American poet, captured the concept with her statement when she said, "Books are more than books. They are the life, the very heart and core of ages past, the reason why men lived and worked and died, the essence and quintessence of their lives." Others have spoken of their personal obsession with books, as in Thomas Jefferson's simple statement: "I live for books." But more compelling, perhaps, is the almost instinctive excitement in children for books and stories.

Throughout my years at First Book, I have heard truly extraordinary stories about the power of books in the lives of children. In one case, a homeless child, who had been bounced from one location to another, later resurfaced—and the only possession that he had fought to keep was the book he was given as part of a First Book distribution months earlier. More recently, I met a child who, upon receiving the book he wanted, flashed a big smile and said, "This is my big chance!" These snapshots reveal the true power of books and stories to give hope and change lives.

As these children grow up and continue to develop their love of reading, they will owe a profound debt to those volunteers who reached out to them—a debt that they may repay by reaching out to spark the next generation of readers. But there is a greater debt owed by all of us—a debt to the storytellers, the authors, who have bound us together, inspired our leaders, fueled our civilizations, and helped us put our children to sleep with their heads full of images and ideas.

WHO WROTE THAT? is a series of books dedicated to introducing us to a few of these incredible individuals. While we have almost always honored stories, we have not uniformly honored storytellers. In fact, some of the most important authors have toiled in complete obscurity throughout their lives or have been openly persecuted for the uncomfortable truths that they have laid before us. When confronted with the magnitude of their written work or perhaps the daily grind of our own, we can forget that writers are people. They struggle through the same daily indignities and dental appointments, and they experience the intense joy and bottomless despair that many of us do. Yet somehow they rise above it all to deliver a powerful thread that connects us all. It is a rare honor to have the opportunity that these books provide to share the lives of these extraordinary people. Enjoy.

Green Gables, located in the town of Cavendish on Prince Edward Island, is a popular tourist destination. Each year, thousands of visitors from around the world visit the site that inspired the setting of L.M. Montgomery's tale of a red-haired orphan, Anne of Green Gables. *In addition to the Green Gables House, several museums and sites invite visitors to learn more about Anne and Montgomery, and a popular musical version of the story runs every summer. Tours highlight the heritage of the area and Montgomery's role as an author of national historical significance.*

1

"An Epoch in My Life"

The moment we see our first darling brain-child arrayed in black type is never to be forgotten. It has in it some of the wonderful awe and delight that comes to a mother when she looks for the first time on the face of her first born.

—*L.M. Montgomery,* The Alpine Path

ONE WINTER DAY in 1906, as she was rummaging through a closet, Lucy Maud Montgomery found a hatbox containing a manuscript that she had written a few months earlier. It was the story of an orphan girl named Anne Shirley, who came to live with an elderly couple in a house with green gables.

Although she thought herself a writer, the 31-year-old Montgomery was also the primary caretaker of her elderly grandmother, a responsibility that put her in charge of the upkeep of their antiquated homestead, as well as had her managing its grounds and serving as the town's post-mistress for the post office, which was located in her home. Montgomery and her grandmother lived in Cavendish, a picturesque village on an even more beautiful piece of Canadian seascape, Prince Edward Island. Her days were filled with chores, cooking, nursing, and occasional social-izing when the townspeople stopped by to collect their mail. In the evenings, however, after her regular day's work was complete, Montgomery would sit at the window of her upstairs gabled bedroom and write the articles, stories, and poems that, when published, provided the main source of income for the two women.

Montgomery had been publishing steadily since she was sixteen years old, and had often thought about breaking away from shorter pieces and beginning a book. To write a novel had always been a hope and desire, but Montgomery knew that to do so would be a long and arduous task. Where would she find the time? Her days were devoted to taking care of her grandmother and keeping house; her evenings, to the writing that kept them alive.

As most writers do, Montgomery kept a notebook in which she scribbled ideas and notes from things she had heard or seen. When she was ready to work on a new short story, she would read her jottings for inspiration. In the spring of 1904, as she was searching for an idea for a serial story for a Sunday school newspaper, she came upon a note she had written several years before. It read: "Elderly couple apply to orphan asylum for a boy. By mistake a girl is sent to them."

Still intending to write a serial, Montgomery planned a plot, outlined chapters, and developed the character of Anne, all in the evenings, after a full day of tending to grandmother, house, and grounds. A picture of a young girl in an American magazine was Montgomery's first mental vision of Anne; from this, the character was born, "already christened, even to the all important 'e'." As Montgomery wrote Anne's story, the character seemed to take on a life

Did you know...

One of L.M. Montgomery's earliest pen pals was her cousin, Penzie Macneill, to whom she wrote copiously, especially during the year she was away in Prince Albert, Saskatchewan. In the 1970s, a package of Maud's letters to Penzie was found in the attic of the home of Penzie's son, William Stevenson, in New Glasgow. Stevenson approached Dr. Francis W.P. Bolger, an expert on Prince Edward Island history, to authenticate the letters. In 1974, Dr. Bolger released a book titled *The Years Before Anne*, in which selected pieces of Montgomery's correspondence are found. *The Years Before Anne* is considered one of the most authoritative books on Montgomery because it reveals, in the author's own words, her views on life and the many facets of her coming of age. Montgomery's letters to Penzie Macneill are now housed at the University of Prince Edward Island's Robertson Library.

of her own. "[Anne] soon seemed very real to me and took possession of me to an unusual extent. She appealed to me, and I thought it rather a shame to waste her on an ephemeral little serial. Then the thought came, 'Write a book. You have the central idea. All you need to do is to spread it out over enough chapters to amount to a book'," Montgomery wrote in her autobiography, *The Alpine Path*, published in 1917.[1]

Montgomery began working on *Anne of Green Gables* in the spring of 1904 and finished writing it in October 1905. "[I]n the end, I never deliberately sat down and said 'Go to! Here are pens, paper, ink and plot. Let me write a book.' It really all just 'happened'," Montgomery wrote.[2]

Anne of Green Gables is the story of an outspoken carrot-topped orphan named Anne Shirley, who unexpectedly comes to live with an elderly brother and sister, Marilla and Mathew Cuthbert. The Cuthberts are originally disappointed that they did not get the orphan they had asked for—a boy to help out around their farm. However, as Anne matures into an adolescent and continues her search for "kindred spirits," she melts the elderly siblings' hearts and they eventually come to love her as their own.

When Montgomery finished writing *Anne of Green Gables*, she typed it on an old second-hand typewriter that "never made capitals plain and wouldn't print 'w' at all." She sent it first to a new American publisher, Bobbs-Merrill in Indianapolis. She thought she would have a better opportunity of being published by a newer publisher than by an older one that was better known and already had a list of preferred writers. The manuscript was rejected. Montgomery then submitted it to MacMillan, an established publishing firm in New York City. Now she told herself that an older, more stable company might be more inclined to take a chance on a new writer. The company also rejected *Anne of Green Gables*. She sent it to three "betwixt and between firms," those that were neither new nor very experienced. All sent *Anne of Green Gables* back, with one publisher sending along a letter with the rejected manuscript. "Our readers report that they find some merit in your story," it read, "but not enough to warrant its acceptance."[3]

"That finished me," wrote Montgomery. "I put *Anne* away in an old hat-box in the clothes room, resolving that some day when I had time, I would take her and reduce her to the original seven chapters of her first incarnation. In that case I was tolerably sure of getting thirty-five dollars for her at least, and perhaps even forty."[4]

Montgomery forgot about *Anne of Green Gables*, then came across it by accident one day. As she reread her book, she thought it didn't seem so bad and decided to start submitting it to publishers once again. She retyped it on a better typewriter, making a few revisions as she did. Then Montgomery submitted *Anne of Green Gables* to the L.C. Page Company, a publishing company located in Boston owned by two brothers, Lewis and George Page.

"The book may or may not succeed. I wrote it for love, not money, but very often such books are the most successful," Montgomery wrote in her journal while waiting to hear from the Page brothers about the fate of her book.[5] To Montgomery's surprise, not only did the L.C. Page Company offer to publish *Anne of Green Gables* and pay her a 10% royalty on the wholesale price of each book, they also asked her to immediately begin working on a sequel.

Anne of Green Gables was published in 1908. Within five months, it had gone through six printings, selling 19,000 copies. Montgomery's first royalty check in 1909 was for $1,730. In a journal entry of February 1910,

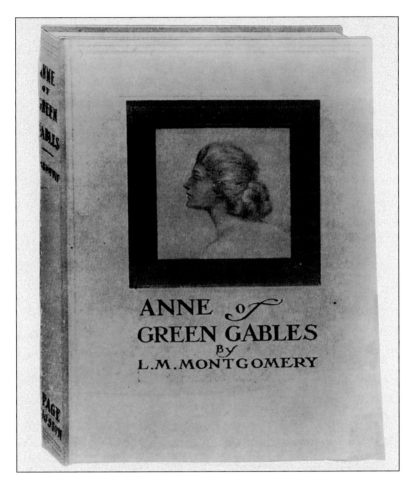

The original cover for L.M. Montgomery's Anne of Green Gables, *first published in 1908. The young woman has her hair styled in the "Gibson Girl" fashion—upswept at the top and caught close to the neck. The Gibson Girl, an idealized woman of the early 1900s, was the creation of Charles Davis Gibson, a prolific illustrator for popular magazines. Spirited and independent, yet feminine, the Gibson Girl was much like Montgomery's heroine Anne Shirley.*

Montgomery wrote that in Anne's first year alone, she earned $7,000. This was at a time when the average yearly income for a woman on Prince Edward Island was $300.

On June 20, 1908, Montgomery held her first copy of *Anne of Green Gables*. On that day she recorded the following words in her journal: "My book came to-day, fresh-new from the publishers. I candidly confess that it was to me a proud, wonderful and thrilling moment. There, in my hand, lay the material realization of all the dreams and hopes and ambitions and struggles of my whole conscious existence—my first book. Not a great book at all, but *mine, mine, mine*, something to which *I* had given birth—something which, but for me, would never have existed."[6]

Montgomery's dream of writing a book, born when she was but a schoolgirl and nourished by years of heartache and sadness, had at last come true. It was, as Anne Shirley herself would say, "an epoch in my life."

Lucy Maud Montgomery at eight years of age. Early on, Montgomery recognized that her vivid imagination set her apart from other children. She received a rigid and strict upbringing from her maternal grandparents, who raised Montgomery after her mother's death. She invented imaginary friends and developed a rich fantasy life to help ease the loneliness of her childhood.

2

"Little Maudie"

The incidents and environment of my childhood . . . had a marked influence on the development of my literary gift . . . . Were it not for those Cavendish years, I do not think Anne of Green Gables *would ever have been written.*

—*L.M. Montgomery,* The Alpine Path

LUCY MAUD MONTGOMERY was born in the small village of Clifton, now known as New London, on the north shore of Prince Edward Island on November 30, 1874. Named after Edward, duke of Kent and father of Queen Victoria, Prince Edward Island remains one of Canada's most

19

picturesque provinces. It is also the smallest Canadian province and is in some places a mere three miles wide. Its coastline is dotted with bays and coves; further inland, the rich, red soil complements the many shades of the green rolling countryside.

The French explorer Jacques Cartier first set foot on *Abeqweit*, the name given to Prince Edward Island by the natives, in 1534. *Abeqweit* means "Floating on the Wave," a fitting way to describe the Island's abundant vegetation, which lies cradled on all sides by the turquoise shimmer of the Gulf of the Saint Lawrence River. Today, inhabitants call their island "The Garden of the Gulf." "You never know what peace is until you walk on the shores or in the fields or along the winding red roads of *Abeqweit* on a summer twilight. . . . You will find your soul then," Montgomery wrote.[1] Throughout her life she would seek inspiration and consolation in the natural beauty of her birthplace.

Montgomery was born into a family that had been well established on Prince Edward Island for over 100 years. In the 1700s, the island's rich, fertile soil began attracting colonists from Scotland, Ireland, and England. Montgomery's mother's family, the Macneills, came from Scotland in 1775 and was one of the first three families to settle in Cavendish, a small farming community on Prince Edward Island's northern shore. Montgomery's ancestors also came from England; her maternal grandmother had been born in Dunwich in the county of Suffolk.

The Macneills were a proud family who believed their role as early colonists gave them higher social status than the average Prince Edward Island citizen. They expressed their pride in political activity. Montgomery's great-grandfather, William Macneill, who claimed to be the first male child born in the Prince Edward Island capital of Charlottetown, was known as "Old Speaker Macneill." He was a member of the Prince Edward Island House of Assembly from 1814–1834, and served as Speaker of the House for the last four of those years. William married into the Townsend family. The family had been gifted a parcel of Prince Edward Island land by King George III, which they named Park Corner, after the family estate in England.

The Macneills believed in education and encouraged reading, poetry recitation, and storytelling among family members. Two of Montgomery's great uncles were writers; one was a satirist, the other a poet. Of her Grandfather Macneill, Montgomery said he was a man of strong and pure literary tastes, who also had a knack for writing prose.

Montgomery never tired of listening to the family stories that had originated in Scotland and were passed along from generation to generation. She often said that she had inherited her love of reading and her gift of writing from the Macneill side of the family. One of Montgomery's favorite relatives was her Aunt Mary Lawson, whom Montgomery considered "one of the formative influences of my childhood. She was a brilliant conversationalist, and it was a treat to get Aunt Mary started on tales and recollections of her youth."[2] In time, many of Montgomery's family yarns and tales made their way into her own short stories and books.

Montgomery was fond of saying she was raised between "Puritan Macneill conscience" and the "hot Montgomery blood." She traced her paternal heritage to the Norman Invasion by William the Conqueror in 1066.

Originally from Normandy, France, the Montgomerys moved to Scotland after the invasion. Family legend placed the Montgomerys on Prince Edward Island by happenstance. The story handed down through the generations told of Montgomery's great-great-grandparents, Hugh and Mary Montgomery, who were bound for Quebec from Scotland. Mary became violently seasick on the voyage. When the ship docked on the north shore of Prince Edward Island to pick up fresh water, Mary went ashore. Despite the pleas of her husband, she refused to reboard the ship. Hence the settling of the Montgomerys on Prince Edward Island.

Hugh and Mary's son, Donald, was Montgomery's great-grandfather. His son, Donald, Montgomery's paternal grandfather, was a Canadian senator and one of the first to represent Prince Edward Island after it joined the Canadian Confederacy in 1873. Montgomery's father, Hugh John, was the oldest of the eight children born to Donald and his wife, Nancy. Hugh John had been a sea captain who had once sailed to England, South America, and the West Indies. He married Clara Macneill when she was twenty-one years old and he was thirty-three. After his marriage, he quit the sea and took up shopkeeping, opening a store called Clifton House adjacent to his home. When their only child, a daughter, was born, they named her Lucy after her maternal grandmother, Lucy Woolner Macneill, and Maud, possibly after a grandchild of Queen Victoria's, Princess Maud of Great Britain, who was born in 1869.

Hugh John called his baby daughter "my little Maudie." Montgomery never used her first name, Lucy, and preferred instead, to be called "Maud without an e." After she became an established author, Montgomery wrote under the name "L.M. Montgomery."

Montgomery's father traveled extensively on business, and when Clara became sick with tuberculosis, both she and little Maudie moved into the Macneill family home in Cavendish. Clara died when Montgomery was not quite two years old. Montgomery attributed her earliest memory to seeing her mother in her casket and touching her cold cheek. "The chill of Mother's face had frightened me; I turned and put my arms appealingly about Father's neck and he kissed me." Montgomery recalled.[3]

After her mother's death, Montgomery remained with her grandparents, Lucy Woolner Macneill and Alexander Macneill. Eventually Montgomery's father moved to Prince Albert, Saskatchewan (then part of the Northwest Territories), 2,500 miles from Prince Edward Island, and left his little Maudie entirely in the care of his wife's parents, who adopted her.

The Macneills were in their fifties and had raised a family of six children by the time they took over little Maudie's care. Both grandparents were controlling, remote, and unaffectionate, and Montgomery often felt like an outsider, even though she was living with family. The young girl often wondered if she was truly loved or merely taken in by her grandparents out of duty and obligation. Although Montgomery was physically well cared for, she was emotionally starved. Her two pet cats, Catkin and Pussy-willow, became substitutes for the lack of human warmth. These were the first of many cats that would bring Montgomery joy throughout her life.

To ease her loneliness, Montgomery often escaped into a world of dreams and fantasy, and even as a very young girl, she possessed a wild imagination. When she was about five years old, Montgomery invented imaginary friends to compensate for her lack of real friends. She gave names like "Little Syrup" to the trees in the nearby orchards and named her geranium plant "Bonny."

Montgomery realized very early on that she was "different" from other children and that it was her vivid imagination that set her apart. Two of Montgomery's imaginary playmates lived in a cabinet with two glass doors. Behind one door lived Katie Maurice, who was Montgomery's age. Behind the other lived a widow named Lucy Gray. Montgomery liked Katie Maurice best, because she was younger and livelier, but she had many conversations with both friends. Knowing her grandparents wouldn't approve of her imaginary friends, she kept them to herself.

The Macneill home was a large farmhouse, and although it lacked electricity and was cold and drafty in the winter, Montgomery loved it and found it comfortable. During the winter months, she slept downstairs. In the warmer months, Montgomery had the use of two small upstairs bedrooms. One served as a playroom, the other as her summer bedroom. This is the room she was later to call her "white and peaceful den," where through her writing, the world was introduced to the people and places of her stories. Montgomery occupied this bedroom until she was thirty-six years old.

When Montgomery entered school at age six, she could already read and write. She wrote in her autobiography that she didn't remember learning these skills and thought perhaps she had been born with them, just as we are born knowing how to breathe and eat. When her teacher realized she could read, Montgomery was skipped over the most basic reading textbook, the "First Reader," and started on the more advanced "Second Reader." Montgomery always felt she had missed an important part of her

L.M. Montgomery's bedroom in her grandparents' house, the Macneill home. She called this her "white and peaceful den," and she occupied this bedroom until she was thirty-six years old. The bedroom is where she created the people and places of her many novels.

education because she had skipped the First Reader. Even as an adult and established writer she "seemed to have missed something, to suffer, in my own estimation . . . a certain loss of standing because I had never had it." Montgomery wrote of "a queer regret in my soul over missing that First Reader."[4]

Montgomery was a temperamental child who easily expressed her emotions. She was also sensitive and did not like to be teased or made fun of. One day when she forgot to take off her hat in school, her fellow classmates laughed at her. Of this incident Montgomery wrote: "I felt that I was a target for the ridicule of the universe. Never, I felt certain, could I live down such a dreadful mistake. I crept out to take off my hat, a crushed morsel of humanity."[5]

The rigid and strict upbringing she received from her grandparents also set her apart from her classmates. While the other students brought their lunch to school and played together at mealtime, Montgomery's grand-mother insisted she walk home for her noon meal. Only on stormy winter days was she allowed to bring her lunch to school. While her classmates went to school barefoot, Montgomery had to wear buttoned boots. Perhaps the most humiliating experience the sensitive young girl had to endure was being forced to wear a new style of apron over her school dress. Grandmother Macneill made the apron, which fit Montgomery like a sack. It also had sleeves—an unheard of style for an apron in those days. The apron was the source of much teasing from her classmates, who called it a "baby apron."

Even her schoolteachers picked on Montgomery, selecting her for extra recitation and cruel taunts. What made this especially hard to deal with was that one of her schoolteachers, Miss Izzie Robinson, boarded at the Macneill's. During the times when her sensitive feelings were hurt, Montgomery would turn to nature to reclaim herself. The one-room Cavendish schoolhouse was located just outside the Macneill property, near a spruce grove and a brook with a cool spring. "That old spruce grove . . . was a fairy realm of beauty and romance to my childish imagination. I shall always be thankful that my school was near a grove . . . it was a stronger and better educative influence in my life than the lessons learned at the desk in the school house," Montgomery wrote.[6] Prince Edward Island's hills, ponds, wildflowers, and apple orchards also soothed the hurt feelings of the sensitive young girl. She found special solace in the coastline, which she came to love in all of its moods.

When she was seven years old, two orphan brothers came to live at the Macneill home. Wellington (called Well) and David Nelson lived with the Macneills for three years. Lucy and the brothers became inseparable and spent summer days fishing, picnicking, picking berries, exploring nearby fields, and building a playhouse near the apple orchards on the Macneill property. They planted a small garden. They named a spruce grove in the field below the orchard "The Haunted Woods" and vied for who could tell the scariest ghost stories. ("The Haunted Woods" as well as many other aspects of Montgomery's imagination would reappear in *Anne of Green Gables* and other books.) They spent winter evenings by the fire doing homework, playing quiet games, and reading. Then, when Montgomery was ten, the brothers suddenly, and without explanation, were gone. Once again, Montgomery found herself a lonely only child.

The one activity that brought Montgomery pleasure was the occasional trip to Charlottetown and the once or twice a year visit to the coastal village of Park Corner, thirteen miles from Cavendish, where her paternal grandfather, Senator Donald Montgomery, "a dearest old soul," lived.

One of Montgomery's mother's sisters, Annie Campbell, also lived in Park Corner with her husband, Uncle John, and Montgomery's four cousins: Clara, Stella, George, and Frederica. Montgomery loved to visit the Campbell's big white farmhouse surrounded by orchards. There one of her wishes was fulfilled, if only temporarily, and she was part of a big, happy, loving family. Montgomery later recreated the Campbell house in two books: *Pat of Silver Bush* and *Mistress Pat: A Novel of Silver Bush*.

The Macneills were Presbyterian and attended the Cavendish Presbyterian Church. The church filled both spiritual and social needs. Montgomery attended Sunday school and enjoyed it much more than church services. "Some of my sweetest memories are of the hours spent in that old church with my little mates, with our testaments

Did you know...

The setting for L.M. Montgomery's books *Pat of Silver Bush* and *Mistress Pat* was the large airy farmhouse in Park Corner where her mother's sister, Aunt Annie, and her husband Uncle John lived with their four children. Built in 1872, it was a solid white house trimmed with green and surrounded by apple orchards and maple and birch trees. Montgomery called it Silver Bush in her novels because when the wind blew, the silvery undersides of the maple leaves would turn upside down and become visible. Montgomery and Reverend Ewan Macdonald were married in the front room of the house in Park Corner; today, couples from all over the world honor their favorite author by exchanging wedding vows in the very same room.

and lesson sheets held in our cotton-gloved hands," Montgomery wrote.[7] The Bible stories and sermons Montgomery heard as a child in church also served to sharpen her adult storytelling abilities.

There appears to have been nothing in Montgomery's early days to provide a clue as to the prolific author she would one day become. Of her childhood Montgomery wrote, "Some might think it dull. But life never held for me a dull moment. I had, in my vivid imagination, a passport to the geography of Fairyland. In a twinkling I could—and did—whisk myself into regions of wonderful adventures, unhampered by any restrictions of time or place."[8]

Wedding picture of L.M. Montgomery's father, Hugh John Montgomery, and his second wife, Mary Ann McRae, in 1887. A few years after the marriage, Montgomery went to live with them in Saskatchewan. Although Montgomery always felt close to her father, she did not get along very well with her stepmother, and after about a year she returned to live with her grandparents on Prince Edward Island. Nevertheless, she did have many happy times in Saskatchewan with her "darling father" and her friends Laura and Will Pritchard.

The Story Girl

There were many traditions and tales on both sides of the family, to which, as a child, I listened with delight while my elders talked them over around winter firesides. The romance of them was in my blood.
—L.M. Montgomery, The Alpine Path

ONE OF THE most exciting events of Montgomery's childhood occurred on July 25, 1883, when she was eight years old. That summer, the *Marco Polo*, a famous old ship that had once been the fastest sailing vessel of her class, was wrecked on the Cavendish coast. The three-masted clipper had sailed out of Quebec destined for Europe with a load of timber when she was caught in a storm in the Gulf of St. Lawrence. Her pumps could not hold back the rush of water, and her captain ran her ashore in order to save the crew and cargo.

For the rest of the summer, the twenty international crew-members of the *Marco Polo* boarded with Cavendish families. The ship's Norwegian captain boarded with the Macneills.

The story of the ill-fated *Marco Polo* was told and retold in the Macneill home, which, as the town post office, also served as a meeting place where neighbors shared village gossip and sea captains came together to dramatize their experiences with storms at sea and ship wrecks. Montgomery sat mesmerized as they told their tales. Of all that she heard, it was the story of the wreck of the *Marco Polo* that impressed her the most. One of her first pieces of recognized writing was an essay entitled "The Wreck of the *Marco Polo*," written for a national contest. The story stayed with her for life, and as an adult, Montgomery often told about the *Marco Polo* when asked to speak at events.

As Montgomery grew into a young woman, life with Grandmother and Grandfather Macneill became more complicated. Her grandparents found it difficult to keep up with Montgomery's adolescent energy. They liked quiet and orderliness, and dissuaded her from bringing friends home. As Montgomery grew into her teens, her grandparents became even more protective and discouraged her from socializing altogether. In his old age, Grandfather Macneill became more unbending and inflexible in his granddaughter's upbringing. He grew increasingly bad tempered and often verbally ridiculed Montgomery, encouraging other family members to do so as well. Without parents to protect her, Montgomery was at the mercy of her grandparents and her aunts and uncles. She was not even allowed to defend herself against their verbal abuses. Although grateful that her grandparents had provided her a home, Montgomery held a lifelong belief that old people should not raise young children.

Montgomery's father visited Cavendish as often as he could, but sometimes years passed between visits. In 1887, Hugh John took a second wife, Mary Ann McRae, who was from Ontario. Mary Anne was the niece of Sir William Mackenzie, a Canadian railroad developer and a designer of the Canadian Northern Railway. The couple soon had a daughter whom they named Kate. Although she hardly knew him, Montgomery missed her "darling father" and longed for a time when she could be reunited with him.

As she grew older, Montgomery escaped her unhappy home life by spending time alone. She took long walks and spent hours reading. Among her favorite authors were Walter Scott, Charles Dickens, William Thackery, and the Brontë sisters. Montgomery read and reread the two red-covered volumes of *A History of the World*. These books, which had simple illustrations, spanned time from Adam and Eve through Queen Victoria. "As history, they were rather poor stuff, but as story books they were very interesting," she remembered.[1] She memorized whole chapters of Scott's *Rob Roy* and Dickens's *The Pickwick Papers*, two of the novels Grandmother and Grandfather Macneill owned. She also enjoyed reading the poetry of Longfellow, Whittier, Milton, and Burns. On Sundays, reading was restricted to the Bible or other religious books. Montgomery's favorite Sunday book was *The Memoir of Anzonetta Peters*. Anzonetta was a child who did everything right yet still met tragedy and misfortune in her life, which she joyfully accepted. When Anzonetta talked, she spoke Biblical phrases, which Montgomery referred to as "talking scripture."

When Montgomery was thirteen years old, a lending library was established in Cavendish by the Literary Society.

Although her grandparents initially forbade her to join the "Literary," they eventually relented, and Montgomery attended the many talks, debates, and presentations that the organization offered. In time, she would call the "Literary" one of the most influential and significant experiences of her life.

Montgomery's favorite subject in school was composition; she did not care for mathematics or history. "You don't find me calling history delicious," she said when she was fifteen years old.[2] She expressed her love of writing when she began keeping a journal as "a tot of nine." By the time she was fourteen, she had grown critical of what she had written and destroyed the journal. In 1889, Montgomery began a second journal, the one she would keep until shortly before her death in 1942. "Life is beginning to get interesting to me," she wrote in her first entry on September 21. From this point forward, Montgomery faithfully recorded all important events of her life. Sometimes she would "journalize" in a smaller notebook, and later recopy what she had written into her main journal.

Over time, the keeping of a journal would prove to be a significant part of Montgomery's life. As an adult writer, she would turn to what she had written in her early years to keep in touch with her youth and provide inspiration for her many books and short stories. Much of what Montgomery wrote was inspired by the people and places she knew personally and about whom she wrote in her journal.

Around the same time that Montgomery started keeping a journal, she wrote her first poem, "Autumn." Its first few lines read:

Now autumn comes, laden with peach and pear;
The sportsman's horn is heard throughout the land,
And the poor partridge, fluttering, falls dead.

By this time, Montgomery had begun writing stories as well, using the backs of discarded printed mail for paper. Some of her early works were morose and gruesome; in these early stories, just about everyone died a bloody and gory death. She also wrote descriptions of her favorite places, biographies of her cats, detailed accounts of school events, and critiques of the books she read.

"I cannot remember the time when I was not writing, or when I did not mean to be an author," Montgomery wrote in 1917. "To write has always been my central purpose around which every effort and hope and ambition of my life has grouped itself. I was an indefatigable little scribbler, and stacks of manuscripts . . . bore testimony to the same."[3]

When she was twelve years old, Montgomery wrote a poem entitled "Evening Dreams." Miss Izzie Robinson, the schoolteacher who boarded at the Macneills, was also a singer, and one evening, using the ruse that her poem was a song, Montgomery asked the woman if she had ever heard of it. With a quivering voice, Montgomery recited the first two stanzas:

> When the evening sun is setting
> > Quietly in the west,
> In a halo of rainbow glory,
> > I sit me down to rest.
>
> I forget the present and future,
> > I live over the past once more,
> As I see before me crowding
> > The beautiful days of yore.

Miss Robinson honestly admitted she had never heard the song, but commented that the words were very pretty.

Montgomery was thrilled. "It was the sweetest morsel of commendation that had ever fallen to my lot, or that ever has fallen since. . . . Nothing has ever surpassed that delicious moment. I ran out of the house—it wasn't big enough to contain my joy . . . and danced down the lane under the birches in a frenzy of delight, hugging to my heart the remembrance of those words," she wrote.[4]

Encouraged by Miss Robinson's favorable remarks, Montgomery copied "Evening Dreams" on good paper and made her first submission ever to a printed publication, but when *The Household*, an American publication, rejected "Evening Dreams," Montgomery was stunned, and it took her a year to recover. Thinking she would have better luck with a publication closer to home, Montgomery sent "Evening Dreams" to a Prince Edward Island newspaper, The Charlottetown *Examiner*. It, too, rejected Montgomery's poem.

"I was crushed in the very dust of humiliation and I had no hope of rising again. I burned my 'Evening Dreams,' and although I continued to write because I couldn't help it, I sent no more poems to the editors," Montgomery said, of her early experiences as a writer.[5]

When she wasn't going to school or writing, Montgomery acted in shows at Cavendish Hall; one of her most notable roles was that of the lead character in "The Fairy Queen." She also spent time with her cousin, Amanda Macneill. The two girls had nicknames for one another. Montgomery was "Polly" and Amanda was "Molly." The girls spent time with two boys, John Laird, whom the girls called "Snap," and Nate Lockhart, whom they called "Snip." Montgomery and Nate had a lot in common. They were both good students who enjoyed discussing books and competing in tough academic subjects, especially against each other. They also liked to play baseball. Nate's feelings towards Montgomery grew from friendship to love, and according to her early journal, she was serious about him as well. Once he expressed his love for her, however, Montgomery grew cold towards him and felt he had spoiled their friendship by falling in love with her.

Just a few months later, in the summer of 1890, Montgomery turned her attention from Nate and towards her father. One of her fondest wishes came true. She was to accompany Grandfather Montgomery by train to Prince Albert in Saskatchewan, where she would stay for an extended visit with her father and his new family. At the time, Prince Albert was still a frontier, and Montgomery's father, known as Monty, held positions as a town developer, auctioneer, forest ranger, and real estate agent, among many others. He had built a fine home, which he named "Eglintoune Villa" after an estate in England once owned by his family. Monty was well known in Prince Albert, and he and his wife had an active social life in the town. In 1891 he was elected to the Prince Albert Town Council. Shortly thereafter he ran in a federal election and lost.

That there would be trouble living with father's new family became apparent shortly after Montgomery arrived. On August 23 she wrote, "[T]o speak plainly, I am afraid I am *not* going to like his wife. I came here prepared to love her warmly and look upon her as a real mother, but I fear it will prove impossible." Montgomery saw her stepmother as having "a dreadful disposition," and found her "sulky, jealous, underhanded and *mean*. . . . I *know* I am not going to be happy here. I have been as nice and respectful to her as I could be but already I find myself disliking and fearing her, and that is not a pleasant prospect."[6]

On the other hand, Montgomery's father showed her great affection. "His eyes just *shine* with love when he looks at me.

I never saw anyone look at me with such eyes before," she wrote in the same journal entry.[7] Montgomery felt sorry for her father, whom Mary Ann "picks and nags at . . . unceasingly." In a later journal entry she wrote that her father admitted that he found it hard to get along with his wife and asked his daughter to put up with the situation for his sake.

"I *cannot* bear the way she uses father. He is so good and kind to her as he is to everybody, and there isn't a shadow of justification for the way she behaves—unless the fact that he is not rich is a justification. She seems to resent that most bitterly," Montgomery entered into her journal on August 26.[8] Eventually Montgomery resorted to calling her stepmother "Mrs. Montgomery," except in the presence of others, when she called her "mama," out of respect for her father. "He has enough to bear as it is," she wrote.[9]

Montgomery's family situation went from bad to worse after January 1891, when her stepmother gave birth to Montgomery's half-brother, Donald Bruce. Now Mary Ann made the young girl do much of the housework, as well as take care of Kate and the baby. It was obvious that Mary Ann thought her stepdaughter could be of use in just one way: as household help. This came at the expense of Montgomery's education, since Mary Ann's reliance on her caused her to miss school for two months.

Despite the tensions within the home, Montgomery had some happy moments. She participated in church concerts and taught Sunday school. She became friends with a schoolmate, Laura Pritchard, and her brother Will. Montgomery and Laura became confidants. Montgomery felt she could tell Laura everything, even her innermost thoughts, and considered her friend her "twin spirit in every way." The young people went tobogganing in the winter and played cricket, went for walks by the river, and picnicked in the warmer months. Will fell in love with Montgomery and throughout her life, Montgomery was to think of him as her closest male friend. They corresponded until his death in 1897.

While in Prince Albert, Montgomery was the recipient of unwanted attention by her teacher, John Mustard, who regularly came to the Montgomery home for unannounced visits. Montgomery called him "that detestable Mustard," and on April 20, 1891, she wrote in her journal, "I hate to be alone with Mustard! I must admit that his attentions are becoming rather serious. All the town is talking about them. I am teased to distraction about him and all sorts of jokes on his name are fired off at me. Even father can't ask me to pass the mustard at the table without a grin! It simply makes me furious!"[10]

Throughout the spring and early summer of 1891, Mr. Mustard continued to call on Montgomery. At last he

Did you know...

L.M. Montgomery did not officially see herself as a feminist, yet she took a uniquely feminist approach to all she did. When her publisher, the L.C. Page Company, threatened to withhold royalties owed on previously published works, Maud hired a lawyer and took them to court—and won. This was considered an unusual and most unladylike action for a woman in the early 20th century. Montgomery's feminist attitudes were also seen in other areas. Working as the lone female at the Halifax *Daily Echo*, using her maiden name professionally, and keeping her income separate from her husband's were also ways Montgomery showed she was a fiercely independent woman.

asked her if she felt there could be a deepened relationship between the two. It was only after definitively telling him no that Mr. Mustard left for Knox College in Toronto to study to become a minister.

In late 1890, Montgomery wrote a poem titled "On Cape Leforce," about a Prince Edward Island legend, and mailed it back home to Charlottetown to *The Daily Patriot*. In school, under the schoolmaster's "suspicious eye" and in the "agonies of homesickness," Montgomery had put to rhyme the story of an eighteenth-century buccaneer who was shot by his mate as the two were preparing to duel over their spoils. The captain was buried on the spot where he died, and the headland was named "Cape Leforce."

On December 7, 1890, Montgomery learned that *The Daily Patriot* had published "On Cape Leforce." On that day Montgomery wrote:

> . . . [T]his has been the proudest day of my life! I feel at least three inches taller than I did yesterday. . . . To-day when I came down, ready for Sunday School father came in with last night's mail and among it a *Patriot*. I seized it with a beating heart and trembling fingers and opened it. I grew dizzy—the letters danced before my eyes and I felt a curious sensation of choking—for there in one of the columns was my poem! I was just too delighted to speak. Father was so pleased and I am so glad and elated and happy. I can't find words to express my feelings.[11]

Montgomery continued to see her name in print throughout that winter and the following summer. A poem entitled "June" was also published in *The Daily Patriot*, and "Farewell" was published in the Prince Albert *Saskatchewan*. The Prince Albert *Times* printed her description of Saskatchewan, an essay called "A Western Eden." However, it was her 1,600-word prize-winning essay about the ill-fated

View of Cape Leforce in Cavendish, Prince Edward Island. In November 1890, when Montgomery was living with her father in Saskatchewan, she wrote a poem called "On Cape Leforce," the story of an eighteenth-century buccaneer. She sent the poem to a Prince Edward Island newspaper called The Daily Patriot. *The newspaper accepted it, and Montgomery had her first poem published in December 1890, when she was sixteen years old.*

Marco Polo that brought her the most recognition. Entitled "The Wreck of the Marco Polo," the essay was awarded a prize by the Montreal *Witness* and in 1891 was reprinted in an anthology, *Canadian Prize Stories.*

Homesickness and Mary Ann's rejection prompted Montgomery to return to Prince Edward Island in August 1891. Although the year had been filled with heartache, Montgomery was glad she had come. She had spent a whole year with "darling father," whom she was never to see again. She had made good friends, traveled, and seen a good deal of Canada. But by far the brightest spot of the year was getting published. When she had left Prince Edward Island for Saskatchewan, she had been a teenaged schoolgirl. It was as a published writer that she returned.

L.M. Montgomery, seated in the front, and three of her schoolmates, as students at the Prince of Wales College in Charlottetown, Prince Edward Island. Montgomery received First Class Honors in five subjects and Second Class Honors in three. She called her year at the Prince of Wales College the happiest of her life.

4

Miss Montgomery, the Teacher

I really believe I am learning to like teaching. But this week has seemed as long as a year.

—L.M. Montgomery, journal, August 3, 1894

BACK ON PRINCE Edward Island, Montgomery stayed with her Aunt Annie and Uncle John Campbell in the big farmhouse in Park Corner. In the year she had been away, Montgomery had grown into a striking young woman. She was of average height, yet dainty. Her once golden hair had darkened to a soft brown and hung to her knees. The freckles she had as a child had faded away, and her eyes changed from

43

gray to blue. Montgomery felt her small hands were her best features; the thing she disliked the most about herself was her mouth. She felt that it was too small.

Montgomery spent the year giving music lessons to her cousins and writing verses for *The Daily Patriot*. She also wrote an account of her trip back home to Prince Edward Island, which *The Daily Patriot* published.

Although she knew in her heart that she was destined to be a writer, she also knew how difficult it was, especially for a woman, to make a living in her chosen profession. In mid-1892, Montgomery applied to the Prince of Wales College in Charlottetown, twenty-four miles from Cavendish, to earn a teacher's license. To prepare for the entrance examinations in English, French, Latin, geometry, and algebra, Montgomery returned to the Cavendish school for an additional year. The extra study paid off; Montgomery finished fifth in the entrance exam out of 264 candidates. When the test scores were printed in the *Charlottetown Daily Patriot* on July 15, 1893, her ranking made her "the happiest girl in Cavendish."

Once Montgomery arrived at Prince of Wales College, she sent another poem, "The Violet's Spell," to *The Ladies World*, a New York magazine. Her payment was two subscriptions to the magazine, the first compensation of any kind that she had received for her writing.

"It's a start and I mean to keep on," she wrote in her journal around this time. "Oh, I wonder if I shall ever be able to do anything worth while in the way of writing. It is my dearest ambition." [1]

Montgomery was not alone at Prince of Wales College; she had as her roommate her third cousin, Mary Campbell. The girls shared a big front room a few blocks from the college in a boardinghouse run by a Mrs. MacMillan.

Although Montgomery immersed herself in studying for her teacher's certificate, she did attend services and other activities at the Zion Presbyterian Church, as well as write for the college newspaper, *The College Record*.

Because she needed to become a teacher—and to have an income—as quickly as possible, Montgomery studied 18 subjects in one year, a course load that normally took two years to complete. Her overloaded schedule often had her attending classes with second-year students who knew one another and did not take kindly to the newcomer. In spite of her accelerated pace, Montgomery received First Class Honors in five subjects and Second Class Honors in three. Each year at the Prince of Wales commencement

Did you know...

L.M. Montgomery considered the year she spent studying for a teacher's license at Prince of Wales College the "happiest of my life." Always keeping her academic objectives in sight, Montgomery also took advantage of the active social life Charlottetown offered. Freed from the watchful eyes of her grandparents, Montgomery and her many cousins also studying in Charlottetown went to football games, attended church revivals, and spent many hours in the city's waterfront Victoria Park, where Montgomery would tell the others stories. Montgomery found the park to be a pretty place, and it reminded her of being home in Cavendish.

ceremony, one student was selected to read an original essay. That year Montgomery was chosen to read "Portia— A Study," which was also reprinted in the Charlottetown *Guardian* to critical acclaim. Montgomery called her year at the Prince of Wales College in Charlottetown the happiest of her life.

Three days after graduation, Montgomery began five days of grueling exams for her teacher's license, and on June 18, 1894, she returned to Cavendish, to await the results. Out of 120 students, only 49 passed, and Montgomery had placed sixth. Her joy in receiving her teacher's license, however, was eclipsed by the resistance she encountered from Grandfather Macneill. He was of "the old school" and believed a woman needed neither education nor career, and would do nothing to help his granddaughter achieve her goals. "I can not get to apply to the trustees in person and so I have a poor chance," Montgomery wrote on July 13, 1894. "Other girls' fathers or friends drive them about to apply for schools but grand-father will not do this for me, or let me have a horse to go myself, so there is nothing for it but letters, which are generally not even answered." [2]

Later that same month, however, nineteen-year-old Montgomery was offered a job in Bideford, a fishing village in the northwestern part of the Island, about 66 miles from Cavendish. Montgomery began her career as a teacher on July 30, 1894. She boarded in the comfortable and hospitable home of a Methodist minister and his wife. Her first class in the one-room schoolhouse initially consisted of twenty students but soon swelled to thirty-eight, and as her first full year of teaching came to an end, Montgomery was responsible for an overwhelming sixty pupils. A mixture of homesickness for Cavendish and lack of self-confidence at first gave Montgomery serious doubts about her ability to teach, but her negativity was short-lived. By the end of the summer her self-doubts were gone, and she was performing well in her new profession. When she left Bideford, she said she would always think kindly of her year there.

Despite a heavy student load in Bideford, Montgomery continued to write, using the pen name, "Maud Cavendish." She published a poem and a story entitled "A Baking of Gingersnaps" in the Toronto *Ladies Journal*, as well as a few other pieces here and there, although much of her writing was rejected by the magazines and newspaper to which it was sent. She told no one of her "ambitions and failures." Of this time Montgomery wrote:

> At first I used to feel dreadfully hurt when a story or poem over which I had laboured and agonized came back, with one of those icy little rejection slips. Tears of disappointment *would* come in spite of myself, as I crept away to hide the poor, crimpled manuscript in the depths of my trunk. But after a while I got hardened to it and did not mind. I only set my teeth and said "I will succeed." I believed in myself and I struggled on alone, in secrecy and silence. . . . Down, deep down, under all discouragement and rebuff, I knew I would "arrive" some day." [3]

Although she was teaching, Montgomery was still focused on becoming a writer and wanted to do all she could to succeed. She believed that studying English literature would help her become a better writer, and when her year in Bideford was up, she decided to take a year off from teaching. Returning to Cavendish, she tried to persuade Grandfather Macneill to pay for a year of schooling at Dalhousie University in Halifax, the capital of Nova Scotia. As expected, the old man was strongly opposed to Montgomery continuing her education. Working as a teacher had provided her with enough income to cover half the expenses of a year at Dalhousie. In spite of her husband's resistance, Grandmother Macneill covered the remaining half of Montgomery's expenses, and in the autumn of 1895, Montgomery entered Dalhousie University.

Montgomery knew she could not afford to study for a bachelor's degree, but wanted instead to take selected courses that would help her with her writing and understanding of literature as a whole. At first Montgomery found Dalhousie difficult. She was also battling poor health, and in one year she was stricken with the measles, the flu, and several colds. Also, at twenty-one years old, she was quite a bit older than her fellow students were. Having been a teacher herself, it was difficult for her to follow the rules and regulations designed for the younger women at the Halifax Ladies College, where the females who attended Dalhousie boarded. Nevertheless, Montgomery studied German, French, Roman history, and Latin, and she took two courses of English literature. She contributed to the university newspaper, the Dalhousie *College Observer*, and two larger Halifax newspapers, the *Evening Mail* and the *Herald.* To earn extra spending money, she gave organ lessons.

While at Dalhousie University, Montgomery received the first monetary payment for her writing. A check for $5 came from an American children's publication called *Golden Days* for a short story. That very same week she received two additional checks: one for $5 from a Halifax newspaper, the *Evening Mail*, for an essay on "Which has greater patience—man or woman," and a $12 check from the popular American weekly magazine for children, *Youth's Companion*. Instead of purchasing such necessary items as boots and gloves with her earnings, Montgomery acquired a five-volume set of poetry that included the works of Tennyson, Byron, and Whittier. She wanted something that would hold forever the moment when she "arrived" as a writer.

Despite her continued publication of short stories and poems in American publications such as *Golden Days*, *Youth's Companion*, and the Chicago daily newspaper, *Inter-Ocean*, her income was not sufficient to continue at Dalhousie University, and after only one year, she left to find work again as a teacher. Edwin Simpson, Montgomery's third cousin, had been teaching in Belmont, a small village about forty miles from Cavendish, and was planning to go to theology school to prepare to become a Baptist minister. He arranged for Montgomery to take over his position at the Belmont school for the winter of 1896–1897.

Montgomery found Belmont to be "a wretched old hole" and the students "stupid, ignorant and rough."[4] Part of her dislike for her position stemmed from boarding with a crude, ignorant, and untidy family named Fraser. The Fraser home was uncomfortably cold and at times snow drifted into her bedroom through the cracks in the walls. Still, Montgomery continued the practice she had begun in Bideford; each morning she rose early and wrote for one hour before going off to teach her students. It was around this time that Montgomery began writing under the name "L.M. Montgomery." Wearing her heavy coat, sitting on her feet to keep them from freezing, and with fingers so cold she could barely hold her pen, the disciplined Montgomery would write her required one hour a

L.M. Montgomery with the students of the Belmont school, around 1897. This was her second teaching position after leaving Prince of Wales College. It was also around this time that Montgomery began writing under the name "L.M. Montgomery." The following year, however, Montgomery did not return to Belmont, but accepted instead a teaching position in Lower Bedeque on the south shore of Prince Edward Island.

day. Then she would warm herself, eat breakfast, and go off to teach.

Later in life Montgomery wrote, "When people say to me, as they occasionally do, 'Oh, how I envy you your gift, how I wish I could write as you do,' I am inclined to wonder, with some inward amusement, how much they would have envied me on those dark, cold winter mornings of my apprenticeship."[5]

The only bright spot in Montgomery's year in Belmont were the Sundays spent with her cousins, Samuel and Eliza Simpson, and their family. In addition to Edwin, whom Montgomery had replaced at the school, the Simpsons had two other sons, Fulton and Alfred. Over time, all three Simpson brothers fell in love with Montgomery, but it was Edwin who asked her to marry him. Although Montgomery did not love him and was not physically attracted to him, she felt they were intellectually well matched. Despite being of different religions—he a Baptist and she a Presbyterian—Montgomery accepted his proposal and the two became secretly engaged. Very soon after, she realized she had made a mistake in agreeing to become his wife, but she was afraid to tell him so.

When school ended, Montgomery returned to Cavendish. The following year she did not return to Belmont, but accepted instead, a teaching position in Lower Bedeque on the south shore of Prince Edward Island. It was a six-month position while the former teacher returned to college. There were only fourteen students in the district, and she found them to be intelligent. She boarded at the home of a family named Leard, whose oldest son, twenty-six-year-old Herman, was a farmer.

Montgomery was attracted to Herman and soon found herself in love with him and powerless to fight her feelings for him. The two kissed in the darkened farmhouse after the rest of the family had gone to bed. Intellectually Montgomery knew that she and Herman were incompatible and that their relationship was a mistake. For one thing, Herman did not approve of Montgomery's desires to be a writer. Montgomery considered Herman intellectually inferior to her. To complicate the relationship even further, Montgomery was still secretly engaged to Edwin Simpson, who visited her at the Leard's, and sent letters and gifts to her there as well.

To Montgomery, who risked becoming a spinster schoolteacher if she did not accept either suitor, there were advantages and disadvantages of both relationships. According to Montgomery scholars Mary Rubio and Elizabeth Waterston:

> If Montgomery accepted Edwin Simpson, as a husband, she would probably have to leave Prince Edward Island; if she chose Herman, she would remain on an Island farm. Ed confidently looked forward to a distinguished career and to powerful influence over his parishioners; Herman, at twenty-six, was permanently settled into the small Lower Bedeque community. Physical contact with Ed left her cold and distressed; Herman's kisses triggered a flooding, passionate response. . . . She knew Ed's sharp—often too sharp intellect would stimulate, arouse and irritate her into intellectual response, while Herman's educational limitations would perhaps curtail her chances of mental and aesthetic growth. The choice would be a binding one: there was no divorce on the Island, and no chance, once married, of resisting the dominance of either minister or farmer.[6]

Montgomery felt there was only one way to resolve her dilemma: stop seeing both men. After many attempts, in the spring of 1898 she broke off her relationship with Herman. Around the same time she sent a letter to Edwin Simpson breaking off their engagement. Edwin eventually became a pastor of a church in Chicago. For ten years, he held on to the hope that Montgomery would reconsider and agree to become his wife; he finally married another woman in 1908.

Montgomery turned to writing to assuage her feelings of romantic hopelessness. Between 1897 and 1898, the author published nineteen short stories and fourteen poems. Montgomery longed to write "fun for fun's sake" stories for young people, but much of her writings from this time were "potboilers," romance stories fictionalized to the point of being unbelievable. The stories she did write for children had to include a moral. "They won't sell without it as a rule," she wrote in her autobiography. Montgomery knew her work fell short of the standards for classical literature, and she longed to be free to write for the joy and pleasure of writing and not only for the income it would bring.

L.M. Montgomery took this self-portrait in her bedroom in the MacNeill home in Cavendish. The photo was taken several years after she returned to the farmhouse to care for her grandmother. In 1898, her grandfather had died, specifying in his will that his wife could live in the house for as long as she could maintain it. In order to remain in her home, Grandmother MacNeill needed Montgomery to take care of her and the major household chores. She was to live there for the next thirteen years.

5

Newspaperwoman!

I never expect to be famous. I merely want to have a recognized place among good workers in my chosen profession. That, I honestly believe, is happiness, and the harder to win the sweeter and more lasting when won.

—*L.M. Montgomery,* The Alpine Path

MONTGOMERY WAS LATER to call the turbulent and chaotic years approaching the turn of the century, the years from hell. In the midst of her confusion about her love relationships, word reached her in Lower Bedeque in March 1898 that her Grandfather Macneill had died suddenly of a heart attack.

Alexander Macneill had left his farm and home to his son, John F. Macneill, whose own property bordered that of his father's. Grandfather Macneill's will specified that his wife, Lucy, could live in the house as long as she could maintain it. John knew that she was unable to maintain it alone and, eager to join his father's land with his own holdings, refused to help his mother. In order to keep her house, Grandmother Macneill needed Montgomery to give up teaching and come back to live with her in the farmhouse. The tides had changed. At one time Montgomery had been in need of her grandmother's help; now her grandmother needed hers. When the school year was over, twenty-four-year-old Montgomery repaid her obligation by moving back to Cavendish to help her grandmother. She would never teach again.

Back at the homestead, Montgomery's world extended no further than the farmhouse and the town of Cavendish. She took care of her grandmother and all the major chores around the house. In addition, Montgomery had to serve as the town's postmistress, as the post office was still located in the Macneill's home. Montgomery's life became a never-ending circle of housekeeping, caretaking, and service to her church, where she played the organ for services. To relax she took long walks. And yet, despite constant interruptions, Montgomery was able to adhere to a writing schedule.

The busy days helped to keep Montgomery's thoughts off of Herman Leard. But she still cared for him, and in September 1898, Montgomery returned to Lower Bedeque to see him. She was testing herself and her feelings for him. The trip showed her what her heart knew all along: she still loved Herman. That visit was the last time she would see him alive, for in the spring of

1899, Herman died of influenza. To a friend, Montgomery wrote: "This man died, and I have always been thankful that it ended so; because if he had lived I daresay I couldn't have helped marrying him and it would have been a most disastrous union."[1] And yet, Montgomery realized that Herman had affected her life in positive ways as well. He had "enriched and deepened my life. *I wouldn't have missed* that *experience* to be a saint in heaven!!" she continued.

When Montgomery's father died of pneumonia in 1900, so soon after Herman's death, Montgomery fell into a depression and was unable to write for weeks. Montgomery's father had always supported her writing career and was the only one who valued and treasured her gift, if but from a distance. Montgomery felt his loss acutely.

Montgomery was eventually able to rouse herself and return to her writing, and by 1901, she it was generating a "livable" income which was enough to support the household. During this time, short stories as well as poetry continued to be Montgomery's main writing genres. One of the reasons Montgomery was so successful in having her work published is that she thoroughly studied the markets she wished to submit to. A steady stream of newspapers and magazines passed through the front room post office of the Macneill farmhouse, giving Montgomery a wide exposure to many publications. Having read them, she knew the type of writing they accepted, then carefully wrote her stories to match the publications.

Montgomery followed the standard themes of early twentieth-century writers and wrote about the unexpected in love, family, and fortune. As one biographer has stated, "[Montgomery] wrote what people wanted to read. She adapted material to the form or formula that would sell.[2]

Not every short story Montgomery wrote was accepted for publication outright. If a manuscript was returned, it was immediately sent out to another publication. In this manner, short stories that were rejected by one publication were eventually published by another. Occasionally a publication would publish one of Montgomery's stories after it had been originally published elsewhere. This brought in additional income.

In 1901, Montgomery's cousin, Prescott, a son of her Uncle John, agreed to take care of their grandmother over the winter months. This break from caretaking left

Did you know...

Among L.M. Montgomery's many interests and activities was creating scrapbooks. During her life she created nineteen books, which contained short stories, poems, and memorabilia such as photographs, newspaper clippings, invitations, pressed flowers, and bits of fur belonging to her many cats. Her first scrapbook was completed in 1893 and contained many items that she had been saving from previous years, including a copy of the invitation to her father's wedding on April 5, 1987. Montgomery referred to her scrapbooks for inspiration when writing her many novels. Today, Montgomery's numerous scrapbooks are housed at the L.M. Montgomery Birthplace on Prince Edward Island and at the University of Guelph in Ontario.

Montgomery free to move to Halifax and take a temporary job as a proofreader and editor for the *Daily Echo*. The time away from Cavendish infused Montgomery's writing with vitality and resulted in an increase in her writing productivity.

A diary entry from November 11, 1901, reads, "I am here alone in the office of the *Daily Echo*. The paper has gone to press and the extra proofs have not yet begun to come down. Overhead, in the composing room, they are rolling machines and making a diabolical noise. Outside of the window the engine exhaust is puffing furiously. In the inner office two reporters are having a wrangle. And here sit I— the *Echo* proof-reader and general handy-man. Quite a 'presto change' from last entry. I'm a newspaperwoman!"[3]

Montgomery had her own weekly column on food and fashion called "Around the Tea-Table," which she wrote under the pen name "Cynthia." She also had to create "society letters" for the newspaper's society page when they weren't submitted by the correspondents in time. The society letters were newspaper columns listing parties and other events attended by the well-to-do. Sometimes she had to make up happy events when there wasn't enough material to fill the society page.

All of the newspaper's odd jobs were given to Montgomery. When a copy of a serial story titled "A Royal Betrayal" was lost, the news editor asked Montgomery to write an end to the tale. What she had read of the narrative thus far did not give her any clue as to how the plot would be resolved. When the serial was published, no one guessed where the initial story ended and Montgomery's took over. "If the original author beholds it, I wonder what he—or she—will think," Montgomery wrote in her journal in December 1901.[4]

More than ten years later, Montgomery discovered a copy of the original story. She was "much amused to discover that the author's development of the plot was about as different from mine as anything could possibly be."[5]

That Christmas, the *Daily Echo* offered a free write-up to any business that advertised with them. Montgomery was given the responsibility of interviewing the business owners and writing up a flattering review of the business. She detested this job, which she performed every afternoon from 3 to 5 P.M. One business, the Bon Marche, was a hat shop. The proprietor told Montgomery he would send a new walking hat over to her if she gave him a good write-up. She thought he was joking, but the day after his review was in the paper, he sent Montgomery over "a very pretty one."

Montgomery's workdays at the paper were so long and challenging that she had difficulty finding the time and energy to concentrate on her own short stories and poetry. She was too tired in the evenings to write, so she tried her heretofore-successful approach of rising early in the morning to write an hour before work. However, she couldn't get to bed early enough to get adequate sleep and wake up refreshed enough to write. Montgomery's only alternative was to write while on duty at the newspaper office. She, who previously required "undisturbed solitude," now found herself writing in the noisy, chaotic environment of machinery running, telephones ringing, and people coming and going. "All my spare time here I write, and not such bad stuff either, since *The Delineator*, the *Smart Set* and *Ainslies'* have taken some of it. I have grown accustomed to stopping in the middle of a paragraph to interview a prowling caller, and to pausing in full career after an elusive rhyme, to read a lot of proof, and snarled-up copy," Montgomery recorded in her journal.[6]

When the temporary job at the *Daily Echo* ended in the spring of 1902, Montgomery's days as a newspaper-woman were over, and she returned home to Cavendish to resume the care of Grandmother Macneill. There she would remain for the next nine years.

L.M. Montgomery met Reverend Ewan Macdonald in 1903, when he came to serve at the Presbyterian Church in Cavendish. They fell in love, and Ewan proposed marriage to Montgomery in 1906. They kept the engagement secret until the death of Montgomery's grandmother in 1911 and they wed shortly after.

6

Anne Comes to Life

I have always hated beginning a story. When I get the first paragraph written I feel as though it were half done. The rest comes easily.
—*L.M. Montgomery,* The Alpine Path

WITH MONTGOMERY'S RETURN to Cavendish came a return to the isolated and quiet life of tending to the house and garden, as well as caring for Grandmother Macneill. Throughout the long years as her grandmother's caretaker, Montgomery's day-to-day activities were subjected to a self-imposed schedule. She cooked, baked, did laundry, and kept house—all without modern-day appliances. In addition to the regular chores,

Montgomery grew fresh vegetables in the summer, then canned them for consumption during the winter months. Since the Macneill house had no electricity, she made candles from the fat of animals slaughtered on the farm.

Grandmother Macneill continued to be difficult and was at times even more demanding and controlling than she had been when Montgomery was growing up. Despite the steadily increasing income Montgomery's writing was providing, Grandmother Macneill carefully watched how much heat, oil, and water was used in the house. She wouldn't allow Montgomery to make any upgrades or improvements to the house either, knowing it would fall into the hands of her son upon her death. And she forbade the hiring of household help to ease her grand-daughter's burden.

Montgomery fell back into the routine she had established before leaving for Halifax. Once the housekeeping chores were taken care of, Montgomery had a bit of time to do the things she wanted to do. Montgomery enjoyed photography, and she not only took pictures of her beloved Prince Edward Island, but also developed them as well, in a small darkroom in the Macneill home. She sewed and embroidered. She was active in the Cavendish Presbyterian Church in many ways, including teaching Sunday school and playing the organ.

One of the things Montgomery enjoyed the most was taking a daily walk around the farm and orchards. As she walked she would "write" stories in her head. Then she would transfer her thoughts to paper in the farm kitchen or in her "white den," the upstairs room that was her bedroom.

Montgomery coped with her isolated existence by writing letters. Miriam Zieber, a writer from Philadelphia with a passion for literature, encouraged the formation of a community of pen pals among writers. Believing "L.M. Montgomery" to be a man, she arranged for Montgomery to begin correspondence with two male writers: Ephraim Weber, who lived in Alberta, and a newspaper reporter, G.B. MacMillan of Scotland. Montgomery would eventually meet both men. Of Weber, Montgomery wrote he had " . . . turned out to be an ideal correspondent. His letters are capital . . . cultured, thoughtful, stimulating epistles to which I look eagerly forward. They are written from a lonely Alberta ranch but they sparkle from beginning to end."[1] In her first letter to MacMillan, Montgomery wrote: "We must feel that we are perfectly free to write as we will, without fear of shocking the other by heresy in any views, spiritual or temporal."[2]

Montgomery corresponded with both men for nearly forty years. As Montgomery's fame grew, Weber asked her for permission to write her biography, which she declined. After her death, he published two articles about her in *The Dalhousie Review*: "L.M. Montgomery as a Letter-Writer" and "L.M. Montgomery's *Anne*."

About the time she was beginning her correspondence with Weber and MacMillan, Montgomery formed a close relationship with Frede Campbell, the daughter of Aunt Annie and Uncle John. Her companionship helped sustain Montgomery during the lonely years when she lived in near-seclusion with her grandmother. The two women remained close until Frede's death in 1919.

If Montgomery felt any unhappiness or discontent at her secluded life as caretaker to her demanding grandmother, she did not outwardly show it. She kept up appearances by being sociable, energetic, and fun loving, although at times she could be sarcastic. She enjoyed going to parties where there was dancing and lively conversation. She loved fashionable clothes and dressing nicely. However, there was another side to Montgomery, one that she did not let others

During her years as caretaker for her grandmother, L.M. Montgomery formed a close relationship with Frede Campbell, the daughter of her Aunt Annie and Uncle John. The friendship helped sustain Montgomery during the many years when she lived in near-seclusion with her grandmother, and the two women remained close until Frede's death in 1919.

easily see. She was often depressed and moody, and suffered from severe headaches. She also went through periods of insomnia and anxiety. Only in her journal, however, did she acknowledge these afflictions.

For the first two years after her return from Halifax, Montgomery concentrated on writing short stories and serials. Her writing ranged from light fiction to ghost stories. A new thought was taking place inside her head, however, and that was to write a book, one that "would live." But she was concerned about taking time away from her "regular" writing—the work that supported both her and her grandmother.

However, Montgomery was unable to abandon her idea of writing about the misplaced orphan girl. She started writing *Anne of Green Gables* on an evening in May 1905 and finished it in October 1905. Nothing she had written prior had given her as much pleasure to write. To Montgomery, Anne was more than a character in a book—she was a live person who had much in common with the author. The most noticeable similarity is that they are both orphans raised by people older than their parents would have been. The sternness of Marilla, the elderly sister, recalls Grandmother and Grandfather Macneill's strict demeanor. In school, Montgomery competed academically with Nate Lockhart. Anne competes in school with Gilbert Blythe. Montgomery and Anne are both nature lovers. The village of Avonlea in *Anne of Green Gables* appears to be strikingly similar to Cavendish. The Haunted Woods in the book are based upon the Haunted Woods that Montgomery played in as a child. The Lover's Lane, a short trail that leads to the ocean in the book, was based on one near the Macneill property. The house with the green gables did indeed exist; it was that of Montgomery's grandfather's cousins, David and Margaret Macneill.

Montgomery's use of real places and events in the creation of *Anne of Green Gables* set a precedent that she would follow in the writing of the rest of her books. Many of them were based upon events that occurred during her life—mostly her difficult childhood and teenage years—or upon stories that had been handed down through the generations and retold by her grandparents or Aunt Mary Lawson. Often Montgomery would reach back through the years by rereading her journals so as to write true the tone of the story, maintain a youthful point of view, and retell events as close to their actual occurrence as possible.

As much like real people as Montgomery's characters appear to be, with one exception (Peg Bowen in *The Story Girl*), the writer denied drawing any of her characters from real people. "I have never . . . met one human being who could, as a whole be put into a book without injuring it," Montgomery wrote, adding that a writer must create characters for them to be believable and lifelike.[3]

Reviewers responded favorably to *Anne of Green Gables*. *The Republic* of Boston called *Anne of Green Gables* "sweet, innocent and fragrant as a branch of apple blossoms."[4] Almost overnight the reclusive woman whom many people had assumed was destined for spinsterhood was thrust into the limelight. Most people from Cavendish were proud of the best-selling author who had put Prince Edward Island on the map. Others failed to see why so such a fuss was being made over Montgomery. She was only a writer, they thought, and after all, it didn't take much talent or energy to write a book. Montgomery realized that people who thought this way would never understand the years of hard work and toil that culminated in writing a book such as *Anne of Green Gables*.

The success of *Anne of Green Gables* far exceeded the aspirations Montgomery had for it. She believed she had written what was then called a "juvenile," a book for young readers. She had teenaged girls mostly in mind when she wrote it, but it soon became apparent that the book had a following of readers who were young and old, as well as male and female. Children saw Anne as a real child who did believable things. Adults enjoyed the book because it reminded them of their own childhood.

Soon the post office of the Macneill house was flooded with letters from people from all over the world tell telling Montgomery how much they enjoyed *Anne of Green Gables*. Sometimes the letters were addressed not to the author, but to her lovable character. One letter was addressed to "Miss Anne Shirley c/o Miss Marilla Cuthbert, Avonlea, P.E.I., Canada, Ontario," but it still found its way to Montgomery. One special letter came from a much-admired writer himself. Mark Twain, the celebrated author of *Tom Sawyer* and *Huckleberry Finn*, called Anne "the dearest and most lovable child in fiction since the immortal Alice [in Wonderland]."[5]

By August 1908, Montgomery had finished her second book, *Anne of Avonlea*, the sequel to *Anne of Green Gables*

Did you know...

Although L.M. Montgomery was best known for her novels, her first writing love was poetry. "My prose sells and so I write it, although I prefer writing verse," she wrote to her pen pal, G.B. MacMillan. Montgomery wrote her first poem when she was nine years old. Because it didn't rhyme, her father told her it didn't sound like poetry. Thereafter, Montgomery wrote her poetry in rhyme. Her first published piece of writing, "On Cape Leforce," published in the Charlottetown *Daily Patriot* while she was in Prince Albert, was a rhyming poem. Montgomery's only book of poetry published in her lifetime, *The Watchman and Other Poems*, was published in 1916.

requested by her publisher, the L.C. Page Company. Its immediate success surprised Montgomery, who always considered *Anne of Green Gables* to be the better of the two.

The writing of *Anne of Green Gables* coincided with another important event in Montgomery's life. In the spring of 1903, a new minister, the Reverend Ewan Macdonald, came to serve at the Presbyterian Church in Cavendish. Of Scottish descent, he had been born on Prince Edward Island and raised on a farm. Like Montgomery, he had attended Prince of Wales College and Dalhousie College before attending seminary at the Presbyterian Theological College in Pine Hill, Nova Scotia.

Church activities brought Montgomery and the minister together, and Ewan was immediately attracted to Montgomery. In 1905 he began living in Cavendish and spending a lot of time at the Macneill home. Montgomery thought he was handsome and she liked that he was educated, although he mostly talked about subjects related to religion and theology. In 1906, Ewan was preparing to leave for the University of Glasgow in Scotland, where he would undertake graduate studies in divinity. Before he left, he asked Montgomery to marry him.

The childhood days Montgomery spent at Park Corner with Aunt Annie and Uncle John and their happy, loving family had instilled in Montgomery a desire for a large family. At thirty-one years of age, Montgomery knew it was unlikely that she would ever find again the passionate love that she had shared with Herman Leard, and to have children without being married was not acceptable on Prince Edward Island in the early 1900s. Montgomery also realized that if she turned Ewan down, another man might not come along. She conditionally accepted, agreeing to an engagement, but not to marriage, until her grandmother died. Thus the engagement was kept secret for five long years, during which time the two saw each other very infrequently.

Montgomery's fame as an author brought her many honors. In 1910, Montgomery met the Honorable Earl Grey, Governor General of Canada, when he visited Prince Edward Island on an official visit. Also in 1910, Montgomery began writing her third full-length book, *The Story Girl*. Of the over twenty books Montgomery was to write in her lifetime, *The Story Girl* was her personal favorite. In this book, the author introduced a new character, Sara Stanley, who told in thirty-two stories many of the myths and tales of Prince Edward Island, as well as the old family legends that were passed down through the generations and told and retold as Montgomery was growing up.

Eager for more books from their newest best-selling author, George and Lewis Page convinced Montgomery to put *The Story Girl* aside and rewrite a full-length serial story originally written in 1907 and titled "Una of the Garden." This was the love story of a man who came to Prince Edward Island from Nova Scotia. The L.C. Page Company published "Una of the Garden" as *Kilmeny of the Orchard*.

Soon after *The Story Girl* was published in 1911, Montgomery visited her publisher in Boston. At the meeting, the Page brothers pressured her to sign a contract that gave them the first option to all work she created during the next five years. Against her better judgment, Montgomery signed the Page's contract.

The Story Girl was the last book Montgomery wrote in the Macneill farmhouse in Cavendish. In 1911, Grandmother Macneill died of pneumonia at the age of eighty-seven, releasing Montgomery from her commitment as caretaker and freeing her to marry Reverand Ewan Macdonald and to move to Ontario to live as his wife.

L.M. Montgomery's son Chester was born in 1912, and son Stuart followed in 1915. Even with two young children, Montgomery held to a strict schedule for her writing. She began writing in the early morning for two hours, during which she was not to be disturbed. The rest of the day she devoted to her boys, Red Cross activities, and church obligations.

7

A Minister's Wife

The trouble seems to be that two people finding themselves harmonious in friendship jump to the conclusion that it will be just the same and even better in marriage.
—L.M. Montgomery, letter to G.B. MacMillan,
April 1, 1907

WITHIN A WEEK after Grandmother Macneill's funeral, Montgomery moved to her Aunt Annie and Uncle John's home in Park Corner. Her grandmother's house was closed up and turned over to Uncle John Macneill, to whom it had been left when Grandfather Macneill died. Although Montgomery would visit the house when she visited Prince Edward Island, no one ever lived in the Macneill house again. Over the years it fell into neglect and ruin, and in 1920 it was torn down. Today a restored foundation marks the birthplace of *Anne of Green Gables.*

Montgomery and Ewan were married at the house in Park Corner in a quiet ceremony on July 5, 1911. Montgomery was thirty-six years old, and Ewan was forty. While her marriage was a long-anticipated occasion, Montgomery had conflicting feelings on her wedding day. "Something in me—something wild and free and untamed—something that Ewan had not tamed—could never tame—something that did not acknowledge him as master——rose up in one frantic protest against the fetters which bound me," she wrote in her journal.[1] These thoughts and feelings attest to the fact that Montgomery was afraid of losing those passionate parts of her personality that allowed her to maintain control of her life.

Montgomery's personal reservations about marriage may have originated with the many life changes she was facing. For many years she had lived a somewhat isolated life, keeping house for her grandmother. Now she was leaving behind the familiar and comfortable: her home, the orchards and woods, the shimmering seashore, and the lush green landscape of her beloved Prince Edward Island. Ahead of her was a new role of minister's wife in a faraway place with a man she barely knew.

The couple sailed from Montreal on the *Megantic* for a ten-week honeymoon to England and Scotland. To visit the British Isles, the land where her ancestors had been born, had been another of Montgomery's dreams. Montgomery used royalty money she had received from her books to pay for their honeymoon. In doing so, she set a precedent. For all the years of her marriage, Montgomery kept her own earnings separate and did not hand them over to Ewan, as was customary for a wife to do at the time. While Ewan worked for the church, they lived rent free, and Ewan's salary supported them. Montgomery used her own money to pay for household help and "extras."

Montgomery planned the honeymoon, scheduling a visit with her pen pal, George B. MacMillan, who showed the newlyweds the Scottish countryside and historic castles. Montgomery was particularly eager to visit the places she had read about in *Ivanhoe* and *The Lady of the Lake*, books written by Sir Walter Scott. In England, Montgomery and Ewan visited the Lake District, where Samuel Taylor Coleridge and William Wadsworth had been inspired to write their poetry. They visited London, the home of two other famous writers, Charles Dickens and William Shakespeare. One of the highlights of the trip was visiting the village of Dunwich, in England's Suffolk County. Here Montgomery saw the small farmhouse where Grandmother Macneill had lived before coming to Prince Edward Island.

On their return trip home, they passed through New York and Toronto to get to Leaskdale, about sixty miles northeast of Toronto. There Ewan held a position as pastor of St. Paul's Presbyterian Churches, in Leaskdale and in the nearby community of Zephyr. Montgomery and Ewan lived in the manse, a home provided for them by the church. In many ways, the manse was to be Montgomery's first real home of her own. She selected paint, carpet, and wallpaper, and had purchased new furniture for all the rooms. Yet the house was not without its faults. For one, it did not have an indoor bathroom. And while there was a spacious minister's study for Ewan, Montgomery had to settle for writing on the dining room table.

The first few years of the Macdonald's marriage appear to have been happy ones. Montgomery quickly acclimated herself to the responsibilities of being a minister's wife. She assisted with the youth groups and Sunday school classes, visited congregation members and attended prayer services. She also attended all weddings, funerals, and baptisms. She entertained members of the congregation. Although she performed her duties as a minister's wife to perfection, yet first and foremost she considered herself a writer. She continued to write under the name "L.M. Montgomery," which was an embarrassment to Ewan, who expected her to follow the established custom of taking his name and calling herself "Mrs. Ewan Macdonald." To pacify Ewan, as well as keep the name she had worked so hard to establish and by which she was known, Montgomery took on two designations. Professionally she was known as "L.M. Montgomery." At the church and in the community of Leaskdale, she was "Mrs. Macdonald."

Shortly after moving into the manse, Montgomery learned she was pregnant. A son, Chester Cameron Macdonald, was born on July 7, 1912, when Montgomery was thirty-seven years old. The pregnancy was an easy one, and she continued to write until the baby was born, finishing *Chronicles of Avonlea*, a collection of previously written stories revised to include Anne Shirley, and *The Golden Road*, a sequel to *The Story Girl*.

A little over a year after Chester's birth, Montgomery was pregnant again. Secretly she hoped the baby was a girl. This time her pregnancy was difficult, and in 1914, Montgomery had to put aside the writing of her third *Anne* book because of complications. On August 13, 1914, a second son, Hugh, was stillborn. Montgomery's deep grief over the loss of the baby was intensified by the knowledge she had wanted a daughter instead of a second son.

Around the same time, World War I erupted in Europe. England and France declared war on Germany, and Canadian volunteers were called up to fight on the side of the Allies. Montgomery became involved in the war effort at home, working with the Red Cross and preparing packages to send to the Canadian soldiers on the front. For a while she served as president of the local Red Cross Society. She followed reports of the war very closely and recorded information about its progress daily in her journal.

In the midst of her personal grief over the loss of her baby, and national sorrow over the war, Montgomery continued to write, and in November 1914, finished *Anne of the Island.* Over the years Montgomery had increasingly turned to her cousin Frede for emotional support. Now she leaned on Frede more than ever to get through this difficult period in her life. Frede was a teacher of Household Science at Macdonald College near Montreal. The college was a day's train ride from Leaskdale, and Frede was a frequent visitor at the manse, often staying for weeks at a time. The youngest of the Campbell cousins of Aunt Annie and Uncle John, and nine years younger than Montgomery, Frede and Montgomery had grown close over the years. Montgomery had even made it financially possible for her younger cousin to attend Macdonald College, where she was now employed. Montgomery considered her cousin her kindred spirit and soul mate. As intelligent, educated, and creative women, the two had much in common besides family.

In the spring of 1915, when Frede became ill with typhoid, Montgomery rushed to Montreal to help her recover. That summer, the two cousins vacationed at Park Corner. It was the first time Montgomery had returned to

Prince Edward Island since her marriage in 1911. The vacation was especially needed, as Montgomery was pregnant once again. Fearful that this baby also would be stillborn, Montgomery was nervous and apprehensive the entire pregnancy. In October of the same year, Montgomery gave birth to a healthy baby, her third son, Ewan Stuart, whom she called Stuart.

With two young sons in tow, and her many responsibilities as a minister's wife, Montgomery reverted to the tried and true writing habit that had been successful for her in the past. She began writing in the early morning for two hours a day behind the closed dining room door. She firmly instructed her sons and the household help that she was not to be disturbed during this time. The rest of the day was devoted to the boys, Red Cross activities, and church obligations. Chester and Stuart became integrated in church activities at an early age. Montgomery took her young sons to church, sitting in the pew reserved for the family of the minister. Like other parents of young children, Montgomery left with them in the middle of the service when they became too noisy.

Montgomery did not find it easy to be a minister's wife. She was by nature a fun-loving person, but as Ewan's wife, she was expected to be quiet and sedate. She was not allowed to dance or outwardly show enjoyment in music. Ewan's full schedule as a minister left him very little time to help Montgomery raise their two sons, and the burden of child rearing fell on her shoulders. Montgomery clearly expressed her unhappiness with her social position when she wrote to George MacMillan: "Those whom the gods wish to destroy they make minister's wives."[2]

Montgomery's normal day-to-day schedule was overwhelming in and of itself, but it was further complicated in 1916 by a series of lawsuits initiated by the L.C. Page Company, which would last for close to a decade. Over the years, Montgomery had grown increasingly unhappy with her publisher, and after the release of *Anne of the Island*, she entered into negotiations with a Canadian publisher, McClelland, Goodchild & Stewart, naming it the primary Canadian publisher of her future works. Montgomery also negotiated contracts with additional publishers in both England and the United States. This angered the Page brothers, who felt they were still entitled to publish Montgomery's books, and they sued her for the rights to publish her future works.

McClelland, Goodchild & Stewart released *Anne's House of Dreams*, which Montgomery had finished in October 1916, and *The Watchman and Other Poems*, a volume of Montgomery's poetry that the L.C. Page Company had rejected because the brothers did not feel there was enough of a market for poetry. The American publisher struck back at Montgomery by withholding $1,000 of her royalties for previous works, claiming they had made a "mistake" in a royalty statement. Montgomery retained an attorney from the American Author's League, of which she was a member, to sue for recovery of her royalties. Montgomery also counter-sued, claiming the L.C. Page Company had sold reprint rights to her writing without her consent.

"I am glad to have succeeded in escaping from their clutches, though I suppose it is at the price of all my old books ought to bring in. They will cheat me out of the profits on them if they can," Montgomery wrote to Ephraim Weber in 1917, shortly after the legal battles had begun.[3]

In the end, the L.C. Page Company was ordered to return the $1,000 to Montgomery, and she, in turn, agreed to sell the publisher the rights to all of her writing heretofore published. It seemed to Montgomery to be the right thing to do at the time, since she was eager to avoid further legal battles. However, it was a poor business decision. Montgomery received only $18,000 for her work, while over the years, the L.C. Page Company earned this figure many times over from book, movie, and stage adaptations of Montgomery's works.

Montgomery continued the saga begun in *Anne of Green Gables* with *Rainbow Valley*, which she finished in 1918. Her joy at its publication the following year was marred by her cousin Frede's death in January 1919 of pneumonia, a complication of influenza. Montgomery mourned the loss of her friend and cousin for the rest of her life. "I do not think that since Frede died there has been one waking hour in which I have not thought of her, or one day in which there has not been, at some moment or other a pang or remembrance that pierced soul and spirit," Montgomery wrote.[4] Soon after Frede's death, Montgomery began *Rilla of Ingleside*, which in many ways paralleled the life of her cousin, friend, and confidant. *Rilla* also centered on the theme of war and how it affects the lives of the women left on the home front.

While the Great War had come to an end, Montgomery's private battles were escalating. For most of his life, Ewan had suffered from depression, insomnia, and melancholia. In 1919, he began experiencing religious delusions in which he was convinced of his predestination to spend eternity in hell. He was diagnosed with a nervous breakdown, and Montgomery sent him to Boston for a consultation with a nerve specialist. Montgomery herself began taking sleeping pills to get enough rest to handle Ewan's situation, her family, church responsibilities, and her writing. Five weeks later, Ewan's condition was pronounced under control, and he returned to Leaskdale. He would, however, fight delusions and depression for the rest of his life, with each recurring delusional episode attacking with greater intensity.

Montgomery shielded the members of Ewan's congregations from the true nature of his mental illness. She made excuses for his "headaches" and called in substitute preachers when needed. He went on "vacations" when he had to be hospitalized and was not able to work. Montgomery never spoke of her husband's illness with others, and she kept his malady so well hidden that not even the house-keepers at the manse guessed that his headaches were really a cover up for his deteriorating mental state. The stress of keeping up the ruse was released only in her journal, at a great expense to her own health.

Anne of Green Gables appeared for the first time as a silent movie in 1919, with dialogue that was important to the plot appearing on the screen. Montgomery was not happy with the production. In the book, the setting is unmistakably Prince Edward Island. The movie, however, did not clearly portray this. An American flag even appeared in one scene. Montgomery also noted that the filmmaker had taken liberties with the story and had included scenes in the movie that Montgomery had not written in the book. In addition, Montgomery thought the child actress who portrayed Anne, Mary Miles Minter, was wrong for the part.

Perhaps Montgomery's biggest disappointment over the movie version of *Anne of Green Gables* had to do with the rights to the story. Montgomery had sold the dramatic rights to the L.C. Page Company to settle the earlier lawsuit, so she would receive no monetary compensation for this movie nor for any other adaptations of her early novels.

In 1920, Montgomery's legal battles with the L.C. Page Company resumed. The publisher was planning to release a collection of Montgomery's short stories written prior to 1912 called *Further Chronicles of Avonlea*. Montgomery had revised the stories, carefully deleting any mention of Anne Shirley, but the L.C. Page Company was intent on publishing the first version, in violation of the earlier court settlement specifying that this book would not contain any reference to *Anne*. Montgomery got an injunction to keep the book from going into print, but *Further Chronicles of Avonlea* went to press, and the Page brothers counter-sued Montgomery for "malicious litigation." This charge was dismissed in 1923 after an appeal to the United States Supreme Court.

Montgomery had yet to taste true victory where the Page brothers were concerned. They appealed to have their suit re-heard, but were denied. Eight months later they took Montgomery to court once again, threatening to seize the royalties owed her by a British publisher. The new libel suit was dismissed and was once again appealed. In 1925 the Massachusetts Supreme Court ruled that the L.C. Page Company had violated an earlier court ruling when it published the unrevised version of *Further Chronicles of Avonlea*, and awarded Montgomery a monetary settlement. From the day it was published, Montgomery refused to consider the pirated book as one of hers. Legalities lingered until 1928, when all of the L.C. Page Company's appeals were exhausted. Montgomery was free of the L.C. Page Company at last. Her stand against the unfair practices of publishers was not only a personal victory, but also one for all writers everywhere.

With the completion of *Rilla of Ingleside* in August 1920 came the end of the *Anne* books. "I am done with

Anne forever. . . . I want to create a new heroine now—she is already in embryo in my mind. Her name is *Emily*," wrote Montgomery in her journal on August 24.

With Frede's death, Ewan's illness, and the prolonged legal battles to contend with, Montgomery was entering one of the most emotionally distressing times of her life. About this period of Montgomery's life, Rubio and Waterston, the editors of Montgomery's journals, have written:

> Montgomery felt increasingly lonely in her private world: Frede was dead, and emotional intimacy was not possible with a husband who lapsed into frequent mental illness and who had no intellectual interests outside of theology. Nevertheless, custom required that she always put on a smiling face for public view. When in August 1921 one parishioner commented that she always seemed so bright and happy, she reacted—though only in the privacy of her journal— "Happy! With my heart wrung as it is! With a constant ache of loneliness in my being! With no one to help me guide and train and control my sons! With my husband at that very moment lying on his bed gazing at the ceiling and worrying over having committed the unpardonable sin!"[5]

In the face of personal adversity, Montgomery continued to write. She started *Emily of New Moon* in August 1921. Like Montgomery, Emily longs to be an author. Montgomery finished the new book in February 1922—less time than it had taken her to write any other book. Two years later, its sequel, *Emily Climbs*, was published.

In 1923, Montgomery was made a Fellow of the Royal Society of Arts of England, becoming the first woman from Canada to receive this honor. Her popularity as an author put her in demand as a speaker, and various organizations throughout North America invited her to speak before their members and to read aloud from her books. Montgomery accepted as many invitations as she could.

The same year, 1923, was also a year of changes in the Presbyterian Church. Members of the General Assembly voted to join with the Methodist Church and the Congregationalists to create a United Church of Canada. A bill authorizing the merger, The Church Union Bill, passed Parliament, but was amended by the Canadian Senate to allow each Presbyterian congregation to vote for itself as to whether it wanted to remain Presbyterian or join with the other denominations. Ewan strongly opposed the merger and worked to persuade the members of both of his congregations to counter it as well. In January 1925, both voted not to merge. His victory, however, had come at a high price, both to his health as well as to his leadership abilities within his congregations, and after nearly fifteen years as the minister in Leaskdale, Ewan decided to seek another position.

It was around this time that Montgomery's writing took a slightly different turn. Before her departure from Leaskdale, Montgomery began writing, *The Blue Castle,* her first novel for adults. *The Blue Castle* is a romance set in Ontario. Written in fits and starts, Montgomery often had to take time away from it so that she could put herself in the proper mood for writing it.

In the winter of 1926, Ewan accepted a position to be a minister at a church in the farming community of Norval, a half-hour's train ride west of Toronto. The move was unsettling to Montgomery, who looked upon the manse in Leaskdale as her one true home. But once the Macdonald family settled in Norval in the red brick manse alongside the church, Ewan's mental state began to improve.

Montgomery once again took up her required church duties. She was active in the Women's Missionary Society Meetings, the Norval Choral Society, and the Women's Institute. She fit in well in the social community as well as the church community. As time went on she adjusted to life in Norval and wrote that she loved the small community as much as she loved Cavendish.

One of Montgomery's special joys was her involvement in the Young People's Group, an organization that presented theatricals and concerts. In addition to directing evenings of entertainment, she sometimes participated by reading from her works. During her first few months in Norval,

Did you know...

Throughout her adult years, L.M. Montgomery was a passionate photographer. She purchased her first camera in the 1890s and took "snaps" of people and places wherever she went. Setting up a darkroom in the Macneill farmhouse, Montgomery learned to develop her own pictures, which at the end of her life numbered in the thousands. The photographic record she left behind allows a glimpse into Montgomery's life from another perspective—behind the camera lens—and permits a study of her world as it looked to her. Montgomery's photographic collection, parts of which were exhibited as recently as 1996, is housed at the University of Guelph in Ontario. Montgomery scholars continue to study the photographs as a way of learning more about the author.

Montgomery continued to work on *Emily's Quest*, the third book in the *Emily* series, which she finished in October 1926. No longer relegated to the dining room to write, Montgomery once again wrote in her bedroom, where she found inspiration in a "hill of pines," which made her reminisce about her childhood.

One of the highlights of Montgomery's early years in Norval occurred in August 1927, when she was presented to Edward, the Prince of Wales and heir to the throne; Prince George; and Stanley Baldwin, the Prime Minister of Great Britain. The men were on a royal visit to Toronto to celebrate the fiftieth anniversary of Canada's confederation. Montgomery spent a good part of the evening discussing books with Prime Minister Baldwin, who told Montgomery repeatedly how much he and his wife enjoyed her writing.

Montgomery was now hard at work on a book titled *Magic for Marigold*. This was an expansion of four short stories about a character named Marigold that Montgomery had been contracted to write for *The Delineator*, an American magazine. Marigold was Montgomery's youngest main character to date. *Magic for Marigold* was published in 1928. New heroines followed in quick succession. Pat Gardiner was the main character of two books, *Pat of Silver Bush* and *Mistress Pat*, and Jane Stuart was that of *Jane of Lantern Hill*.

The year 1929 was a difficult one for Montgomery. Financially, she was affected by the stock market crash in October, and with Chester at college and Stuart at boarding school, Montgomery counted on the income generated by her writing more than ever. She endured a series of minor illnesses—toothaches, earaches, and several episodes of asthma. By 1930, she was well enough to return to Saskatchewan on a speaking tour, where she visited her father's grave for the first time. She also met Laura Pritchard, the "twin spirit" she had befriended forty years earlier when she had visited her father and stepmother. The trip was also momentous for a third reason. Montgomery visited her pen pal of many decades, Ephraim Weber, who was a teacher. Montgomery had met Ephraim briefly when he and his wife had come through Norval. On this visit, Ephraim invited Montgomery to read aloud from her books to his students, who were very familiar with the author and her writing.

Upon her return from Saskatchewan, Montgomery began her second adult novel, *A Tangled Web*. She was also returning to her tangled life.

A scene from the 1934 remake of Anne of Green Gables. *The remake is credited with reawakening interest in the* Anne *books, and L.M. Montgomery completed* Anne of Windy Poplars *in 1935 and* Anne of Ingleside *in 1939. A film of the novel, starring the child actress Mary Miles Minter, was made in 1919, but all prints of the film are believed to be lost. Montgomery was not happy with either the production, which set the novel in America, or the choice of actress for Anne.*

"Journey's End"

For her, writing was a refuge, a solace, and a joy. Luckily she was able to pass her joy along to others. Whatever the tensions of her life, she never lost the ability to turn her experiences and secret dreams into poignantly memorable fiction.

—Mary Rubio and Elizabeth Waterston,
in "Writing a Life," p.13

MONTGOMERY ONCE COMMENTED that 1919 was her last year of happiness, yet throughout her entire life she had to continually grasp at whatever joy she could from a life of heartache and disappointment. A look at the major events in

Montgomery's life—her mother's death and her subsequent rearing by emotionally distant grandparents; the physical abandonment of her father and rejection of her stepmother; the brief passionate romance with Herman Leard that did not, and could not, result in marriage; the forfeiting of the best years of her young adulthood to care for her grandmother; the decade-long legal battles with her publisher; and finally the marriage to a man who progressively became less of a husband and more of a burden—shows that there were few times in Montgomery's life when she was without struggle.

Ewan had a deep affection for Montgomery, and she loved him, but over the years she increasingly realized she had little in common with him. He was shy; she was sociable. They weren't intellectually compatible. He did not enjoy nature and couldn't match her physical energy. The only subject he felt comfortable speaking about was theology. As his mental illness progressed, he stopped providing emotional support to Montgomery, who was shouldering parenting and church obligations in addition to her writing. Her journals from this time illustrate that her devotion to her husband and her sons came at the expense of her writing. Nevertheless, Montgomery was astute enough to realize that in an age when women had few life choices, marriage to Ewan bestowed upon her "the dignity of the matron." At the same time, however, Montgomery felt that being a minister's wife caused her to lead a "life of respectable slavery."

That her marriage was a burden, Montgomery confided only to her diary. There has been much speculation over whether Montgomery would have married Ewan had she known the true progression his mental illness would take over the years. Although as a young minister he recognized he was prone to depression, most likely Ewan himself did not understand what his malady was or the eventual course it could possibly take. In the early part of the twentieth century, mental illness was not as openly discussed as it is today. Furthermore, because medical researchers and doctors were just beginning to understand mental illness as a disease, progressive treatments for it were not available at the time.

One major point of contention in the Macdonald marriage was that Montgomery never felt Ewan respected her writing. He did not read her books and at times appeared to resent her success and popularity, as well as the money she earned. It may very well have been that Ewan was also disappointed in the marriage. His position as a minister required that he have a traditional marriage with a traditional wife. When he proposed marriage to Montgomery in 1906, she was struggling for recognition as a writer. Her role as her grandmother's care taker highlighted many of the qualities that would make Montgomery a good minister's wife. But much had changed over the years, and by the time they married in 1911, Montgomery was a best-selling author, known and loved in Canada as well as the rest of the world, and Ewan had no choice but to share her with her millions of fans.

Whatever he thought of her writing, it is clear that Ewan enjoyed the fruits of her labor, and the extra money it brought into the household. During the later years, when Ewan was unable to work, the McDonalds survived completely on the income generated by Montgomery's writing.

Although Ewan loved his sons, for long stretches of time he left their complete care, including discipline, to his wife. When he was well enough to function, his church duties consumed him, leaving him little time for a normal family life. The two Macdonald sons, Chester and Stuart, were not without their share of problems as they reached young adulthood in the late 1920s. Chester was an engineering student at the University of Toronto, and Stuart was attending boarding school at St. Andrews in Aurora. It was Chester who worried Montgomery the most. In July 1928, she had written that he was involved in "something nasty and worrying" and that she had a "deep-seated fear of his future." By 1930 it was evident that he had become romantically involved with Luella Reid, the daughter of a member of one of the Presbyterian Church's oldest families. Montgomery did not approve of the match. When Chester failed his first year at college, the resulting worries placed additional stress on Montgomery's health, and she had a nervous breakdown that lasted for six weeks.

Midway through Chester's repeat year, he was asked to withdraw from the college because he had failed four courses. He decided to change to a career in law. With his parents' help, he was able to apprentice in a law office, a prerequisite for attending law school. Then, while attending his first year of law school, he gave Montgomery additional reason for anxiety when he secretly married Luella and announced that they were expecting a baby.

Montgomery's younger son, Stuart was a gymnast and had been Ontario's junior champion for two years. He eventually won a national championship in 1935. Academically, however, Stuart was also going through a difficult time. He failed his first year at the University of Toronto Medical School because of lack of attention to his studies.

Montgomery was a forceful presence in her sons' lives and often tried to control the way they lived. At times the anxiety she experienced over her sons caused her to become so distraught that she was unable to write in her journal. The years between 1933 and 1936 were one such time, and Montgomery had to resort instead to scribbling notes whenever she could and incorporating them later into her journal. In the midst of her personal turmoil, however, Montgomery continued to work. She collaborated with two other authors on a book of essays about Canadian women called *Courageous Women*, and in January 1934 she began a sequel to *Pat of Silver Bush*.

During the early 1930s, Ewan's mental health further deteriorated, and he began to lose his memory. He was treated by a succession of doctors in his quest for relief. One of Montgomery's journal jottings for June 1934 mentions that Ewan was undergoing "electric head treatments" and taking blood pressure pills, bromides, and other medication for his mental illness. That same month he was admitted for a three-month stay in Homewood Sanatorium in Guelph. It was around this time that Chester was fired from his law office apprenticeship, providing additional anxiety to his already overwrought mother.

Still Montgomery was driven by necessity to write, and although in 1920 she claimed to be finished writing about Anne, she began another *Anne* book. The remake of *Anne of Green Gables* into another motion picture film by RKO, a Hollywood production company, in 1934 had reawakened interest in the *Anne* books. As she planned out the chapters of the new book, she turned to the earlier *Anne* books to help her recapture Anne's spirit and infuse it into the new book. In late 1935 she completed *Anne of Windy Poplars*. Unlike the original books in the series, *Anne of Windy Poplars* has no plot. Instead, it is a series of chapters, each forming its own self-standing story. Montgomery set the time of the book to fit between *Anne of the Island* and *Anne's House of Dreams*.

Eventually Ewan was unable to work at all as a minister. His deteriorating health combined with the increasing animosity of congregation members over church business forced him to retire from active ministry in 1935. Ewan and Montgomery bought a home on the Humber River in Toronto, which Montgomery named "Journey's End." This home, the last that Montgomery would ever live in, was also the first she had ever owned. To help finance the house, Montgomery sold some of her investments.

After Montgomery and Ewan moved into "Journey's End," both of their sons moved back home. Chester and

Did you know...

L.M. Montgomery's inspiration for Anne Shirley was the vaudeville actress Evelyn Nesbit. Montgomery clipped a picture of Nesbit from an American magazine and looked at it often for inspiration as she wrote *Anne of Green Gables*. In 1906, Nesbit made newspaper headlines when her husband, Harry Thaw, a millionaire, murdered architect Stanford White, Nesbit's lover before her marriage. The original cover of *Anne of Green Gables* pictured a young woman in profile, with hair styled in the "Gibson Girl" fashion—upswept at the top and caught close to the neck—hardly the representation of an orphan. Montgomery had no say in the selection of this depiction, which was approved by her publisher, the L.C. Page Company, and chosen to target young women readers.

Luella had separated, and Stuart had formed a romantic relationship with a woman from Norval that Montgomery did not approve of. From 1935 on, Montgomery periodically succumbed to depression and nervousness that she called her "waves." Life consisted of "awful fits of bottomless despair. They are so dreadful. I cannot describe them. It seems for just a moment that a black empty gulf of terror opened at my feet, and that moment seems like a century. Fortunately it never lasts longer than a moment," she wrote.[1] The same year, however, in between her "waves," Montgomery was named an officer in the Order of the British Empire—an award made in celebration of King George V's silver jubilee. She was given a pin to mark the honor, which she was to wear only in the presence of the King's representative. While she felt privileged to receive the award, at the same time she was amused and wondered if the King had ever heard of her before bestowing this honor. Montgomery was also elected to the Literary and Artistic Institute of France.

Chester continued to have marital problems. He and his wife reconciled and, despite a shaky marriage, they had another child, a son named Cameron. Around the same time, Chester also became romantically involved with a woman from Toronto. Again, Montgomery was overwhelmed with emotional anxiety. Despite her nervous exhaustion, Montgomery finished *Jane of Lantern Hill*, and tried to come up with an idea for a new book. "If I could get an idea [for a new book] I might gather the material for it while waiting for a return of mental calm," she wrote in her journal.[2]

But mental calm was elusive. Ewan's mental illness resurfaced in 1937, and more than a year passed before she could find the time, emotional stability, and peace of mind to begin *Anne of Ingleside*. She began to write again on September 12, 1938, but less than two weeks later, she was emotionally spent. "Tried to write but had to give up and go to bed," she wrote in her journal on September 27, 1938.[3]

Montgomery's emotional health was intensified by the news from Europe of the growing threat of Hitler. She knew that her sons would most likely be called up for duty should there be a war. In 1938, Chester joined the 48th Highlanders Reserve, but was excluded for active service because of poor eyesight. Stuart was exempt from military duty while in medical school.

Despite Ewan's deteriorating mental condition and several accidents and falls of her own in 1938, Montgomery eventually finished *Anne of Ingleside*. This, her final book, was published in 1939. Soon after, Montgomery sold the movie rights to *Anne of Windy Poplars* and *Anne's House of Dreams* to RKO. Montgomery used the money to purchase a law partnership for Chester. He had received a law degree in 1939, the same year that Stuart received a medical degree.

Marriage and motherhood brought Montgomery much unrest, yet she wrote that she did not regret her decision to marry Ewan, since she loved him and enjoyed being a wife and mother. And while she had just cause to have Ewan permanently committed to a mental institution, she did not, preferring instead to care for him at home, for she knew know one would look after him or understand him as she could.

Montgomery visited her beloved Prince Edward Island for the last time in 1939. Another accidental fall in the spring of 1940 injured her arm and left her unable to write for four weeks. Depression and a nervous breakdown, from which she never fully recovered, followed. Bedridden and weak, she was barely able to continue her correspondence and write brief quotes in her journal. "Such an end to life. Such suffering and wretchedness," she wrote in July 1941.[4] In her last letter to Ephraim Weber, written in December 1941, she wrote that she didn't believe she would ever be well again.

Montgomery had intended to write a sequel to *Jane of Lantern Hill*, but unable to begin a new book, she instead collected earlier stories written about Anne Shirley into a book that she titled *The Blythes Are Quoted*. It was published posthumously by her son Stuart in 1974 as *The Road to Yesterday*.

By the beginning of 1942, Lucy Maud Montgomery had faded into a shadow of the strong woman she had once been and lost her will to live. She died on April 24, 1942, at the age of sixty-seven. Her funeral was held at Green Gables and she was buried in Hill Cemetery in Cavendish, on Prince Edward Island, in a burial plot that she had herself selected.

Cavendish schools were closed on the afternoon of Montgomery's funeral, and the church was filled to overflowing with mourners. The Reverand John Stirling, the same minister who presided over Montgomery's marriage to Ewan, officiated at the funeral. He read from Montgomery's poem, "The Watchman," and one of her short fiction pieces, "Each in His Own Tongue," from *Chronicles of Avonlea*.

"Among the many important and distinguished names adorning Island history, I do not think any will outshine the star that shone and will continue to shine down through out the ages in Lucy Maud Montgomery," eulogized Dr. Frank Baird, an official of the Presbyterian Church in Canada.[5]

Ewan died the following year in Toronto and was buried alongside his wife. Their graves, within sight of the Gulf of St. Lawrence, overlook Montgomery's beloved Green Gables.

Lucy Maud Montgomery in 1919, at the age of forty-five. She was to call 1919 her last year of happiness. Yet despite a life filled with hardships, sacrifice, and disappointments, Montgomery lived life with whatever joy she could. Her writing brought her a phenomenal amount of success and popularity in her lifetime, and her novels continue to delight readers around the world.

9

The Alpine Path

The "Alpine Path" has been climbed, after many years of toil and endeavor. It was not an easy ascent, but even in the struggle at its hardest there was a delight and a zest known only to those who aspire to the heights.

—Lucy Maud Montgomery, The Alpine Path

WHEN MONTGOMERY WAS a child, she found a poem titled "The Fringed Gentian" in a magazine. The author unknown, its words spoke so forcefully to her that she cut out it out and pasted it on the inside cover of her writing portfolio. One verse in particular was her favorite. It read:

Then whisper, blossom, in thy sleep

How I may upward climb

The Alpine path, so hard, so steep,

That leads to heights sublime;

How I may reach that far-off goal

Of true and honored fame,

And write upon its shining scroll

A woman's humble name.

Much of what we know of Montgomery's own climb up the hard, steep path comes to us from the author herself. Beginning at age fifteen, Montgomery religiously kept a journal that served as her personal outlet and way to release her emotions. "Temperaments such as mine *must* have some outlet, else they become poisoned and morbid by 'consuming their own smoke.' And the only safe outlet is in some record such as this," she wrote in 1910.[1] She called her journal her "grumble book," while at the same time she considered it her "life document," where she recorded an account of the best and worst of her day-to-day experiences.

Montgomery's journals spanned fifty years, comprised ten legal-size volumes and contained almost two million words. They were written between 1889 and 1942. Before she died, Montgomery turned over her journals, which included both handwritten versions as well as those she had typed (and edited), to the care of her son, Dr. E. Stuart Macdonald, as a "sacred trust" and requested that they be published some day. Before his death in 1982, Macdonald donated the journals, his mother's scrapbooks, photo albums, and personal library of 264 books, to the University of Guelph in Ontario.

Mary Henley Rubio, Ph.D., and Elizabeth Waterston, Ph.D., two professors of English at the University of

Guelph, edited Montgomery's journals and published the first volume (1889–1910) in 1985. Three additional volumes were subsequently released. The journals chronicle the life of a woman determined to share her gift of writing with the world.

Looking back from the perspective of nearly one hundred years, the writings of Lucy Maud Montgomery, both fiction as well as journal, provide keen insight into the woman as well as the author. Montgomery lived and wrote in an era that did not recognize a woman's worth much beyond what she could contribute to marriage, children, and home. At the time she was first breaking into print, far fewer female

Did you know...

A research institute devoted to the life and work of Lucy Maud Montgomery is located at the University of Prince Edward Island. The L.M. Montgomery Institute opened in 1993 with a mission to honor Montgomery's achievements as a writer, woman, and resident of Prince Edward Island. The institute designs programs that study Montgomery's life and writing, and has sponsored several international conferences that attract undergraduates, postgraduates, and Montgomery-lovers who want to learn more about the author. An annual English grammar program is offered online through the institute for students who study English through a curriculum based on the life and works of Montgomery.

writers were being published than were men. Recognizing her calling to write early in life, Montgomery was not deterred by the odds.

Montgomery's journals show us that in many ways, her plots parallel her life, for the stories she is most remembered for are about strong girls and women overcoming unusual circumstances. The journals also convey another side of this stoic woman and show us that not only was Montgomery able to rise above personal disappointment and sadness, she worked around it, so as to disturb her creativity as little as possible.

Although she acquired a readership following of both sexes, Montgomery primarily wrote for women, and her books, and most of her hundreds of poems, articles, and short stories, focused on female characters of all ages. Because of this, her writing success challenged the current thought on literary criticism, which dictated that literature enjoyed by women lacked literary merit.

Today many of Montgomery's books are considered classics of children's literature. *Anne of Green Gables* remains the most loved and most well known of all of Montgomery's books. It has been translated into Swedish, Dutch, Polish, Norwegian, Finnish, French, and other languages, as well as into Braille. The rights to the works that Montgomery sold to settle a legal dispute with the L.C. Page Company in 1919 reverted back to her family in 1980, opening up the possibilities for additional recreations of *Anne of Green Gables* and other books. Since the first silent *Anne of Green Gables* movie was released in 1919, Anne has been recreated in further films, a play, a musical, and a television miniseries as well as a ballet. London critics named *Anne of Green Gables: The Musical* as the Best New Musical of 1969, and *The Road to Avonlea* was the most successful television series in Canadian history. In 1998, a television series based on *Emily of New Moon* debuted on Canadian TV.

Montgomery's life and work continues to fascinate academic scholars and everyday readers alike. In 1993, the L.M. Montgomery Institute was founded at the University of Prince Edward Island for the purpose of studying Montgomery's life, times, and writing. The institute sponsors projects and conducts research that keeps Montgomery, and her writing, at the forefront of English literature. The L.M. Montgomery Institute also holds an annual lecture series on Montgomery and celebrates the author's birthday.

Further recognition of Montgomery includes several Canadian stamps issued in honor of Montgomery and Anne. Many Websites devoted to Montgomery, her life, and her heroines can be found on the Internet. In Cavendish, a Lucy Maud Montgomery festival is held annually to recreate the life and cultural times of the author.

In the mid-1930s, the government of Prince Edward Island purchased David and Margaret Macneill's farm-house, the setting for *Anne of Green Gables*, when it fell within the borders of a newly created state park—the Prince Edward Island National Park. Each year thousands of Montgomery's readers flock to this landmark to see for themselves the house in which *Anne of Green Gables* took place.

But perhaps the greatest tribute to Montgomery is found in the joy and pleasure experienced over the last 100 years by each new generation of Montgomery readers. Once, when she was answering a survey that asked her favorite dream, Montgomery answered that she wanted to write a book that would "live." Montgomery's dream has come true. She had climbed the Alpine Path.

CHAPTER 1: "An Epoch In My Life"

1 Montgomery, L.M. *The Alpine Path*, in the University of Pennsylvania Digital Library, (*http://digital.library.upenn.edu/ women/montgomery/alpine/alpine.html*), p. 26.

2 Ibid., p. 26.

3 Ibid., p. 27.

4 Ibid., p. 27.

5 Montgomery, L.M. *The Selected Journals of L.M. Montgomery*, Vol. I., edited by Mary Rubio and Elizabeth Waterston. Toronto: Oxford University Press, 1985, p. 330.

6 Ibid., p. 335.

CHAPTER 2: "Little Maudie"

1 Montgomery, L.M. "The Spirit of Canada," in *The L.M. Montgomery Album*, edited by Kevin McCabe and Alexandra Heilbron. Toronto: Fitzhenry and Whiteside, 1999.

2 Montgomery, *The Alpine Path*, p. 6.

3 Ibid., p. 7.

4 Ibid., p. 13.

5 Ibid., p. 13.

6 Ibid., p. 12.

7 Ibid., p. 27.

8 Ibid., p. 27.

CHAPTER 3: The Story Girl

1 Montgomery, *The Alpine Path*, p. 28.

2 Montgomery, *The Selected Journals of L.M. Montgomery*, Vol. I., p. 3.

3 Montgomery, *The Alpine Path*, p. 30.

4 Ibid., p. 19.

5 Ibid., p. 20.

6 Montgomery, *The Selected Journals of L.M. Montgomery*, Vol. I., p. 29.

7 Ibid., p. 29.

8 Ibid., p.30.

9 Ibid., p. 33.

10 Ibid., p. 48.

11 Ibid., p. 35.

CHAPTER 4: Miss Montgomery, the Teacher

1 Montgomery, *The Selected Journals of L.M. Montgomery*, Vol. I., p. 94.

2 Ibid., p. 114.

3 Montgomery, *The Alpine Path*, p. 21.

4 Quoted in *The L.M. Montgomery Album*, edited by Kevin McCabe and Alexandra Heilbron. Toronto: Fitzhenry and Whiteside, 1999, p. 102.

5 Montgomery, *The Alpine Path*, p. 22.

6 Rubio, Mary, and Elizabeth Waterston. *Writing a Life: L.M. Montgomery*. Toronto: EWC Press, 1995, p. 34.

CHAPTER 5: Newspaperwoman!

1 Bruce, Harry. *Maud: The Life of L.M. Montgomery*. New York: Seal Bantam, 1992, p. 15.

2 Epperly, Elizabeth Rollins. *The Fragrance of Sweet Grass: L.M. Montgomery's Heroines and the Pursuit of Romance*. Toronto: University of Toronto Press, 1992, p. 5.

3 Montgomery, *The Alpine Path*, p. 22.

4 Montgomery, *The Selected Journals of L.M. Montgomery*, Vol. I., p. 273.

5 Montgomery, *The Alpine Path*, p. 24.

6 Ibid., p. 24.

CHAPTER 6: Anne Comes to Life

1 McCabe, Kevin. "L.M. Montgomery and Her Pen-Pals," in *The L.M. Montgomery Album*, edited by Kevin McCabe and Alexandra Heilbron. Toronto: Fitzhenry and Whiteside, 1999, p. 177.

2 Ibid., p. 176.

3 Montgomery, *The Alpine Path*, p. 26.

4 "Miss L.M. Montgomery, Author of *Anne of Green Gables*," quoted in *The L.M. Montgomery Album*, edited by Kevin McCabe and Alexandra Heilbron. Toronto: Fitzhenry and Whiteside, 1999, p. 207.

5 Kajihara, Yuka, "An Influential Anne in Japan," in *The L.M. Montgomery Album*, edited by Kevin McCabe and Alexandra Heilbron. Toronto: Fitzhenry and Whiteside, 1999, p. 437.

CHAPTER 7: A Minister's Wife

1 Montgomery, L.M., *The Selected Journals of L.M. Montgomery,* Vol. II., edited by Mary Rubio and Elizabeth Waterston. Toronto: Oxford University Press, 1987, p. 68.

2 Andronick, Catherine M., *Kindred Spirit.* New York: Atheneum, 1993, p. 109.

3 Hebb, Marion, "LMM and Anne Go to Court," in *The L.M. Montgomery Album*, edited by Kevin McCabe and Alexandra Heilbron. Toronto: Fitzhenry and Whiteside, 1999, p. 291.

4 McCabe, Kevin, "Two Very Necessary People: Frede and Ewen," in *The L.M. Montgomery Album*, edited by Kevin McCabe and Alexandra Heilbron. Toronto: Fitzhenry and Whiteside, 1999, p. 255.

5 Rubio and Waterston, *Writing a Life*, p. 74.

CHAPTER 8: "Journey's End"

1 Rubio and Waterston, *Writing a Life*, p. 103.

2 Ibid., p. 110.

3 Ibid., p. 110.

4 Ibid., p. 115.

5 Wood, Joanne, "A Star and a Stone: Maud and Ewen Macdonald," in *The L.M. Montgomery Album*, edited by Kevin McCabe and Alexandra Heilbron. Toronto: Fitzhenry and Whiteside, 1999, p. 245.

CHAPTER 9: The Alpine Path

1 Montgomery, *The Alpine Path*, p. 2.

1874 **November 30** Lucy Maud Montgomery is born in Clifton, Prince Edward Island.

1876 Montgomery's mother dies. Her father relocates about 3,000 miles away in Saskatchewan. Montgomery's mother's parents take her in and raise her.

1883 Montgomery writes her first poem, "Autumn."

1887 Montgomery's father remarries.

1890 Montgomery travels to Saskatchewan to visit her father and stepmother; her first published poem, "On Cape Leforce," appears in the Charlottetown *Daily Patriot*.

1891 Montgomery returns to Prince Edward Island.

1893–1894 Montgomery attends Prince of Wales College in Charlottetown for teacher training.

1894–1895 Montgomery's first teaching assignment at Bideford, Prince Edward Island.

1895–1896 Montgomery studies English literature at Dalhousie University in Halifax, Nova Scotia.

1896–1897 Montgomery accepts position teaching at Belmont, Prince Edward Island; accepts proposal of marriage from Edwin Simpson.

1897–1898 Montgomery accepts a teaching position at Lower Bedeque, Prince Edward Island; Montgomery falls in love with Herman Leard.

1898 Montgomery breaks engagement with Edwin Simpson; her grandfather dies and she returns to Cavendish to care for her grandmother.

1900 Montgomery's father dies.

1901–1902 Montgomery works at the Halifax *Daily Echo*.

1904 Montgomery begins writing *Anne of Green Gables*.

1906 Montgomery becomes secretly engaged to Reverend Ewan Macdonald.

1908 *Anne of Green Gables* is published.

1910 Reverand Macdonald accepts a position in Ontario, giving him responsibility for two churches in Leaskdale and Zephyr; Montgomery meets the governor general of Canada, Earl Gray; Montgomery visits publisher the L.C. Page Company in Boston.

1911 Montgomery's grandmother dies; Montgomery marries Ewan. She moves with him to Leaskdale, Ontario, where he is in charge of two churches.

1912 Montgomery's first child, Chester Cameron, is born.

1914 Montgomery's second son, Hugh Alexander, is stillborn.

1915 Montgomery's third son, Ewan Stuart, is born.

1917 Montgomery writes her autobiography, *The Alpine Path*, requested by the editors of *Everywoman's World*.

1919 Montgomery's cousin Frede dies.

1920 Legal battles with the L.C. Page Company intensify after the publisher releases unrevised *Further Chronicles of Avonlea*.

1923 Montgomery is made a Fellow of the Royal Society of Arts of England; she is the first woman from Canada to receive this honor.

1926 The Macdonalds move to Norval.

1927 Montgomery is presented to the Prince of Wales, Prince George, and the British prime minister.

1928 Montgomery wins a decade-long lawsuit against the L.C. Page Company, her first publisher.

1930 Montgomery returns to Prince Albert and is reunited with Laura Pritchard, a schoolmate from forty years earlier.

1935 Ewan retires from the ministry, and he and Montgomery purchase a home, which they call "Journey's End"; Montgomery is elected to the Literary and Artistic Institute of France; Montgomery is made an Officer in the Order of the British Empire.

1936 Green Gables becomes part of a national park.

1939 Montgomery visits Prince Edward Island for the last time.

1940 Montgomery injures her arm in a fall and suffers from depression.

1942 **April 24** Montgomery dies in Toronto. She is buried at Cavendish, Prince Edward Island.

ANNE OF GREEN GABLES

In *Anne of Green Gables*, L.M. Montgomery introduced the world to Anne Shirley, a feisty, carrot-topped orphan who is accidentally sent to live with the elderly siblings, Marilla and Mathew Cuthbert. In this, the first in a series of eight *Anne* books, Montgomery takes Anne through adolescence to young womanhood. Although many of Anne's relationships get off to a rocky start, Montgomery writes of how Anne wins the love of the Cuthberts, as well as all of Avonlea.

ANNE OF AVONLEA

When eleven-year-old orphan Anne Shirley arrived in Avonlea, no one would have believed that just five years later, she would be the village school teacher. The adventures of Anne Shirley, Marilla Cuthbert, and the people of Avonlea continue in *Anne of Avonlea,* the sequel to *Anne of Green Gables.* Teacher or not, Anne is as rambunctious as ever as she makes Avonlea's business *her* business. In this book, L.M. Montgomery set the stage for more *Anne* books by beginning the romance between Anne and Gilbert Blythe.

THE STORY GIRL

Of the many books L.M. Montgomery wrote, *The Story Girl* was her favorite. It is also Montgomery's most autobiographical work. As she has her heroine, fourteen year old Sara Stanley, spin her yarns and tell her tales, Montgomery recreates many of the stories Montgomery learned from family members and neighbors while growing up on Prince Edward Island. Montgomery followed *The Story Girl* with a sequel, *The Golden Road.*

CHRONICLES OF AVONLEA

In this book, readers meet some of the other colorful people besides Anne Shirley who live in Avonlea. There is no central plot to this book, and while it is technically not included in the series of eight *Anne* books, *Chronicles of Avonlea* is an entertaining collection of twelve short stories based upon the neighbors and friends Anne lives with, and the events that take place in Avonlea.

THE ALPINE PATH: THE STORY OF MY CAREER

Written in 1917, this autobiographical account of L.M. Montgomery's life discusses her childhood and early writing ambitions. Montgomery wrote *The Alpine Path* at the request of *Everywoman's Magazine*, which first published the narrative as a series of magazine articles. While the book is an excellent recounting of Montgomery's early life and writing, because it was written in mid-career, *The Alpine Path* has its limitations, especially for one who wishes to study the entire scope of Montgomery's life and its influence on her writing career.

EMILY OF NEW MOON

L.M. Montgomery carries on her "orphan" theme in *Emily of New Moon*. Like *The Story Girl*, *Emily of New Moon* contains many autobiographical elements. For one, the protagonist, Emily Byrd Starr, is forced to live with her mother's relatives. And like Montgomery, she also wants to be a writer, an aspiration that begins in *Emily of New Moon,* and is followed in two sequels, *Emily's Quest* and *Emily Climbs.* Similar plot themes and conflicts often have readers comparing *Emily of New Moon* to *Anne of Green Gables*, but the protagonists themselves, Anne and Emily, demonstrate different personality traits that allow each character to stand on her own.

MAGIC FOR MARIGOLD

Because Marigold Lesley was L.M. Montgomery's youngest protagonist, *Magic for Marigold* connected Montgomery to her youngest audience. Although not orphaned, Marigold works through the rites of passage theme that is so familiar in other Montgomery novels, and, like many other Montgomery protagonists, Marigold finds self-understanding in the end.

PAT OF SILVER BUSH

In this, the first of two *Pat* books, L.M. Montgomery uses a new character, Pat Gardiner, to tell yet another timeless tale of a girl coming of age on Prince Edward Island. Pat is not as "colorful" a character as Anne Shirley; as a result, *Pat of Silver Bush* is at times a more serious book than *Anne of Green Gables.* Nevertheless, like Anne Shirley, Montgomery doesn't leave Pat at the brink of young womanhood, but allows her readers the opportunity to see the heroine as a young woman in the sequel, *Mistress Pat.*

1908 *Anne of Green Gables*

1909 *Anne of Avonlea*

1910 *Kilmeny of the Orchard*

1911 *The Story Girl*

1912 *The Chronicles of Avonlea*

1913 *The Golden Road*

1915 *Anne of the Island*

1916 *The Watchman and Other Poems*

1917 *Anne's House of Dreams*

1917 *The Alpine Path*

1919 *Rainbow Valley*

1920 *Further Chronicles of Avonlea*

1920 *Rilla of Ingleside*

1923 *Emily of New Moon*

1925 *Emily Climbs*

1926 *The Blue Castle*

1927 *Emily's Quest*

1929 *Magic for Marigold*

1931 *A Tangled Web*

1933 *Pat of Silver Bush*

1934 *Courageous Women* (co-authored)

1935 *Mistress Pat*

1936 *Anne of Windy Poplars*

1937 *Jane of Lantern Hill*

1939 *Anne of Ingleside*

The following books were published posthumously:

1974 *The Road to Yesterday*

1979 *The Doctor's Sweetheart*

1985 *The Selected Journals*

1987 *The Selected Journals*

1987 *The Poetry of L.M. Montgomery*

1988 *Akin to Anne*

1989 *Along the Shore*

1990 *Among the Shadows*

1991 *After Many Days*

1993 *Against the Odds*

1994 *At the Altar*

1995 *Across the Miles*

1995 *Christmas with Anne*

ANNE SHIRLEY

Anne Shirley is a rambunctious, yet sensitive orphan girl who longs "for a kindred spirit"—someone who will recognize her, respect her and above all else love her. We first meet her in *Anne of Green Gables*, and through a succession of what L.M. Montgomery called her "Anne" books, we are able to follow her life through childhood, adolescence, young adulthood, motherhood, and finally old age. The situations that Anne becomes involved in are at once comical and realistic, and have endeared her to young women for nearly one hundred years.

SARA STANLEY

Sara Stanley appears in *The Story Girl*, the book that L.M. Montgomery called her favorite, and its sequel *The Golden Road*. Sara is a fourteen-year-old with a vivid imagination, which she uses in telling stories. Her listeners are enthralled as they are swept away to magical places by her storytelling.

RILLA BLYTHE

Rilla is the youngest daughter of Anne Shirley and her husband, Gilbert Blythe. Rilla's story is set during World War I and begins at the onset of the war, when she is fifteen years old and planning to spend the next few years in the thralls of teenage romantic love. The war changes her plans, however, and Rilla realizes the importance of self-sacrifice as her wartime efforts on the home front draw from her qualities that she never knew she had.

EMILY BYRD STARR

Emily, like L.M. Montgomery herself, knows from a young age that she is a writer. She endures prejudice and battles the old-fashioned mindset of her relatives and neighbors in her quest to be true to herself. As the series of three Emily books progresses, Emily must decide between her own needs or those of her beau, Teddy.

MARIGOLD LESLEY

Marigold was the youngest character L.M. Montgomery wrote about. She appears in *Magic for Marigold*. Unlike the heroines of the author's earlier books, Marigold has a loving mother and a warm and accepting extended family. But her father died before she was born, and she was named after the woman doctor who saved her life. Marigold is a lonely child who turns to an imaginary friend for company.

PAT GARDINER

Pat Gardiner is the main character in *Pat of Silver Bush* and *Mistress Pat*. She has a deep love of her home, "Silver Bush," and longs to stay there, where things never change. Her self-determination sometimes gets the best of her, and in *Mistress Pat* she must reconsider her decision to stay at Silver Bush when she is forced to choose between her home and romantic love.

JANE STUART

Jane Stuart is the main character in *Jane of Lantern Hill*. She and her mother live in Toronto with her oppressive grandmother. Jane believes her father is dead, but finds he is alive while visiting Prince Edward Island. Showing a remarkable strength of spirit, she sets out to reunite her parents.

Andronick, Catherine M. *Kindred Spirit.* New York: Atheneum, 1993.

Bolger, Francis W.P. *The Years Before Anne.* Halifax: Nimbus Publishing, 1991.

Bruce, Harry. *Maud.* Toronto: Seal Bantam Books, 1992.

Epperly, Elizabeth Rollins. *The Fragrance of Sweet Grass: L.M. Montgomery's Heroines and the Pursuit of Romance.* Toronto: University of Toronto Press, 1992.

Gammel, Irene (ed.). *Making Avonlea: L.M. Montgomery and Popular Culture.* Toronto: University of Toronto Press, 2002.

Montgomery, L.M. *The Alpine Path.* University of Pennsylvania Digital Library. *http://digital.library.upenn.edu/women/montgomery/alpine/alpine.html.*

Montgomery, L.M. *The Selected Journals of L.M. Montgomery,* Vol. I. Mary Rubio and Elizabeth Waterston (eds.). Toronto: Oxford University Press, 1985.

Montgomery, L.M. *The Selected Journals of L.M. Montgomery,* Vol.II. Mary Rubio and Elizabeth Waterston (eds.). Toronto: Oxford University Press, 1987

Montgomery, L.M. *The Selected Journals of L.M. Montgomery,* Vol. III. Mary Rubio and Elizabeth Waterston (eds.), Toronto: Oxford University Press, 1992.

Reimer, Mavis. *Such a Simple Little Tale: Critical Responses to L.M. Montgomery's Anne of Green Gables.* Metuchen, New Jersey: The Scarecrow Press, 1992.

Rubio, Mary, and Elizabeth Waterston. *Writing a Life: L.M. Montgomery.* Toronto: EWC Press, 1995.

BOOKS

Bolger, Francis W.P. *Spirit of Place: Lucy Maud Montgomery and Prince Edward Island*. Toronto: University of Oxford Press, 1983.

Eggleston, Wilfrid. *The Green Gables Letters: From L.M. Montgomery to Ephraim Weber, 1905–1909*. Ontario: Borealis, 2002.

Gillen, Mollie. *Lucy Maud Montgomery*. Toronto: Fitzhenry & Whiteside, 1999.

Gillen, Mollie. *The Wheel of Things: A Biography of Lucy Maud Montgomery*. Toronto: Fitzhenry & Whiteside, 1995.

MacLeod, Elizabeth. *Lucy Maud Montgomery: A Writer's Life*. Toronto: Kids Can Press, 2001.

Montgomery, L.M. *The Poetry of Lucy Maud Montgomery*, ed. by Kevin McCabe and John Ferns. Toronto: Fitzhenry & Whiteside, 1987.

Montgomery, L.M., Francis W.P. Bolger (ed.), and Elizabeth Epperly (ed.). *My Dear Mr. M: Letters to G.B. Macmillan*. Toronto: Fitzhenry & Whiteside Limited, 2003.

http://www.uxbridge.com/people/maud.html
 [Lucy Maud Montgomery Website; Author biography with links and list of published works]

http://www-2.cs.cmu.edu/People/rgs/anne-table.html
 [Anne of Green Gables *online book*]

http://www.upei.ca/~lmmi/
 [Website of L. M. Montgomery Institute]

http://www.gov.pe.ca/
 [Prince Edward Island Website]

http://www.oldpoetry.com/authors
 [Old Poetry.com; Contains links to six of Lucy Maud Montgomery's Poetry]

page:

10: © Jan Butchofsky-Houser/
   CORBIS
16: L.M. Montgomery
   Collection
25: L.M. Montgomery
   Collection
30: L.M. Montgomery
   Collection
41: L.M. Montgomery
   Collection
42: L.M. Montgomery
   Collection
50: L.M. Montgomery
   Collection

54: L.M. Montgomery
   Collection
62: L.M. Montgomery
   Collection
66: L.M. Montgomery
   Collection
72: L.M. Montgomery
   Collection
88: © John Springer Collection/
   CORBIS
98: L.M. Montgomery
   Collection

Cover: L. M. Montgomery Collection

ACKNOWLEDGEMENTS

- *L.M. Montgomery* is a trademark of Heirs of L. M. Montgomery Inc.
- *Anne of Green Gables* and other indicia of "Anne" are trademarks and Canadian official marks of the Anne of Green Gables Licensing Authority Inc.
- Material written by L.M. Montgomery is reproduced here with the permission of David Macdonald, trustee, and Ruth Macdonald, who are the heirs of L.M. Montgomery.
- Photographs from the L.M. Montgomery Collection are reproduced by permission from Archival and Special Collections, University of Guelph Library.

MARYLOU MORANO KJELLE is a freelance writer who lives and works in central New Jersey. She writes a column devoted to children's books, called "The Children's Book Nook," for the *Westfield Leader/Times of Scotch Plains–Fanwood*. She holds an M.S. degree from Rutgers Unversity and teaches reading and writing to college students. Marylou is also the author of eleven nonfiction books, many of them biographies. This is her fourth book for Chelsea House Publishers.